THE

SPIRITUAL MAXIMS

OF

PÈRE GROU.

LONDON:
J. T. HAYES, LYALL PLACE, EATON SQUARE
& 4, HENRIETTA ST., COVENT GARDEN.

LONDON
SWIFT AND CO., REGENT PRESS, KING STREET,
REGENT STREET, W.

THESE "*Maximes Spirituelles*," rough and inelegant, but singularly deep and earnest, are perhaps among the most valuable writings of their experienced author. Widely differing from the ordinary Jesuit teaching of the present day, the spirit of Père Grou is almost identical with that embodied in our sound old English ascetic books, such as the *Scale of Perfection*, *Sancta Sophia*, etc.

The present version is slightly abridged from the original, but the sixth chapter contains a few supplementary pages from the *Intérieur de Jésus*, by the same writer.

S. MARGARET'S, EAST GRINSTED,
Quinquagesima, 1874.

SPIRITUAL MAXIMS.

FIRST MAXIM.

By the ladder of holiness men rise and descend at one and the same time.

"*Now mine eye seeth Thee: wherefore I abhor myself.*"

I.

OF THE KNOWLEDGE OF GOD AND OF SELF.

ALL holiness is contained in two points: knowledge of GOD, and knowledge of self. LORD, make me to know Thee, and to know myself. The prayer is short, but its meaning is infinite. Knowledge of GOD elevates the soul; knowledge of self, humbles it. The former lifts it to the abyss of Divine perfections; the latter sinks it to its own abyss of nothingness and sin. And the great marvel is, that this very knowledge of GOD which lifts man up, humbles him at the same time by the comparison of himself with GOD; and self-knowledge, while it humbles him, lifts him up by necessitating his approach to GOD, as the assuager of his misery.

Marvellous ladder of sanctity, whereon men descend while they ascend, and in the same proportion! For the true elevation of man is inseparable from his true humiliation. The first without the last, is pride; the last without the first, is despairing wretchedness. If self-knowledge did not make him little in his own eyes, what would be the effect upon him of the sublimest knowledge of GOD? He would be lost in the exaltation of his thoughts. Or what would avail the knowledge of his exceeding meanness and misery, if the knowledge of GOD did not counterbalance it? He could only fall into horrible despair. But this twofold knowledge tends to make him holy; for holiness requires him to feel and own that he is nothing in himself, that he receives all things from GOD in the order of nature and of grace, and that he expects all things from Him in the order of glory.

When I speak of the knowledge of GOD, I mean no abstract, ideal knowledge, such as was possessed by the disciples of Pythagoras and Plato. They lost their way in vain and barren speculations, the only effect of which was to increase their pride. The Christian's knowledge of GOD is not an endless course of reasonings on His essence and perfections, like those of a mathematician on the circle and triangle. Many philosophers and theologians, who held grand and noble ideas of the Divine Nature, were none the more virtuous or holy in consequence. But what we ought to know, is, what He has Himself revealed concerning the Blessed TRINITY, and the work of each of its Persons in Creation, Redemption, and Sanctification; His power, providence, holiness, goodness, justice, and love; the extent and multitude of His mercies, the marvellous economy of His grace, the magnificence of His promises and rewards, the terror of His threatenings and the rigour of His chastisements; the worship He requires, the precepts He imposes, the virtues He sets forth as our duty, the motives by which He incites us to their practice; we ought to know, in fact, what He is to us, and what He wills that we should be to Him.

This is the true and useful knowledge of GOD, taught in every page of Holy Scripture, and necessary for all Christians; which cannot be too deeply studied, without which none can become holy, and the substance of which is indispensably necessary to salvation. This should be the great object of reflection, meditation, and prayer for light. Let no man fancy that he can ever know enough, or enter sufficiently into so rich a subject. It is in every sense inexhaustible: the more we discover in it, the more we see there is yet to be discovered. It is an ever-deepening ocean for the navigator: an unattainable mountain height for the traveller, whose scope of vision yet increases with every upward step. The knowledge of GOD grows in us together with our own holiness; both are capable of expanding infinitely; and we must set no bounds to either.

This knowledge is not merely intellectual; it goes straight to the heart; touches it, penetrates, reforms, ennobles, and kindles it with the love of all virtues. He who really knows GOD, cannot fail to possess lively faith, firm hope, ardent love, filial fear, thorough trust, and entire submission. He finds no difficulty in avoiding evil and doing well; he complains of no rigour in GOD's law, but wonders at its mildness, and loves and embraces it in all its fulness; he keeps the precepts, and the counsels too. He contemns earthly things, not judging them worthy of attention; uses them as not abusing them, and, looking not at the things seen, which are temporal, passes swiftly through them towards the things eternal. The sweetest attractions of the world do not tempt him; its dangers do not imperil him; nor do its terrors alarm him. His body is on earth; but his soul is, by thought and desire, in heaven already.

This knowledge is drawn from Holy Scripture, rightly studied. But many men read it without understanding, or understand the letter only, and not the spirit. The sacred writings are the source of all that GOD has been pleased to reveal to us of His essence and perfections, His natural and supernatural works, His designs regarding man, the end He wills him to attain, and the means conducive to that end. Therein we see that GOD is the Beginning of all things, that He governs all, and intends all for His glory, and has done all for Himself, there being no other object possible to him. We see the plan, economy and sequence of religion; and the close connection of the rise and fall of empires with that great subject. To sum up the whole in few words: in Holy Scripture, and therein alone, is to be found all that man need know concerning his salvation, and that can fill his soul with fear and veneration and love of GOD.

This knowledge is to be found, besides, in the writings of the Saints, and in other pious books, which are only expansions of Scripture, and are good in proportion as they express its meaning well and explain it perfectly.

It is to be found above all in immediate intercourse with GOD, by means of prayer and meditation. They looked unto Him, and were lightened, saith the prophet. GOD is light, and in Him is no darkness at all. His presence casts out darkness from the soul that prays. Yes. The soul is better instructed concerning Divine things by prayer alone, than wise men are by all their study. Many simple and unlearned persons, taught in the school of GOD, speak more fitly of Him, more nobly, and fluently, and fervently, than the ablest doctors who, not being men of prayer, speak and write of heavenly things in a dry and painful way, devoid of grandeur, warmth, and feeling.

But besides this knowledge, which may be called luminous, because it belongs to the mind, there is another which consists in feeling alone, and is the portion of the heart. This is something sweeter, stronger, and deeper. It is a certain sense given by GOD of Himself and of His Presence. He seems to say to the soul: Taste and see how gracious the LORD is. The advantage of this knowledge beyond the other is, that it binds the will to GOD much more strongly. Here the soul acts not at all: GOD acts within it, and sets it aglow with a spark of His own bliss.

S. Antony knew GOD after this sort when he complained that the sun rose too early, and put an end to his prayer; and so did S. Francis when he spent whole nights repeating with wonderful delight these words: "My GOD, and my All." This sense of GOD, this experimental knowledge, was the desire of all Saints, and the fruit of their union with Him. If GOD is thus to give Himself to us, we must wholly give ourselves to Him, because He bestows this great grace on none but His best beloved. When, like S. Francis, we have given up all things, when we, too, care for no one and nothing but GOD, then we may as truly and as earnestly say: "My GOD, and my All."

It is quite impossible to explain this sense of

God. What is confined to the heart presents no idea to the mind, and is not to be expressed in words. How could the depth of supernatural things be rendered by words, which are inadequate to represent mere natural affections and feelings? But for him to call such things dreams and fancies, who knows nothing of them, is all the same as to deny the effect of natural love on the heart, because he has not felt it himself. Certainly, this sense of God lifts the soul to a greater height than any illuminative knowledge has the power of doing, and renders it capable of heroic designs and perfect sacrifices.

Self-knowledge is no less precious than the knowledge of God, nor is it less necessary to holiness. If we know ourselves, we do ourselves justice; we think of ourselves exactly as we are; we see ourselves as God sees us. And what does He see? Sin and nothingness; and no more. We have no other possessions of our own: everything else comes from God, and must be attributed to Him. If we know ourselves thus, what must be our humility, and our contempt and hatred of self?

I am absolutely nothing. Throughout eternity I was not, and there was no reason why I should exist, nor why I should be what I am. My existence is the simple effect of God's Will: He bestowed it on me as it pleased Him. He preserves it: if His mighty Hand were not upholding me every moment, I should fall back into nothingness. My soul and body, the good qualities of both, everything estimable or pleasing in me, all comes from God. On that foundation, education did its work; and, all things considered, this very education was rather a gift from

GOD, than the result of my own industry and application.

Not only what I am, but what I have, what I enjoy, what surrounds me, whatever I meet with wherever I go, all comes from GOD, and is for my use. I am nothing: and, except GOD, all else is nothing. What then can I love and esteem in myself or in others? Nothing but what GOD has given. Thence it follows, that in all which is, of itself, nothing, and exists only by the will of GOD, I must only love and esteem GOD and His gifts. And this is a strong foundation of humility and of contempt for self and created things.

But this is not all. I am sin, by my own will, by my abuse of my most excellent gift of liberty. What mean these words, I am sin? In the first place: that in the depths of my nature, and even by my being brought out of nothingness, I have the wretched power of offending GOD, of becoming His enemy, of transgressing His law, of failing in my duty, and of falling short for ever of my true end; and this power is so inherent in me, as a creature, that nothing can part it from me. The power of sinning has, since Adam's fall, become a tendency, and a strong inclination, to sin. By his fault I lost the perfect equilibrium of liberty, in which I should otherwise have been created.

In the second place: that since I have had the use of reason, I have actually sinned; and have been guilty of a great number of offences more or less grievous. Very small is the number of those who have retained their baptismal innocence; and as to venial sins, which are greatly harmful, they are prone to blemish even the highest sanctity.

In the third place: that there is no sin, however enormous, that I cannot commit, if I am not always on my guard, and if God does not preserve me from it. There only needs an opportunity, a temptation, an act of unfaithfulness, to induce the most fearful train of consequences. The greatest Saints believed this of themselves; and we shall not go wrong in believing it of ourselves, after their example.

In the fourth place: being once fallen, I am absolutely unable to rise again in my own strength, or truly to repent of my sin. If God do not open my eyes, move my will, hold out a helping hand, all is over with me; I shall heap up sins, and shun amendment, and harden myself, and die in impenitence; and I have always need to fear this terrible catastrophe, no matter what pitch of virtue I may have reached.

This is not all: my wretched inclination to evil is united to an equal distaste for all things good.

All law is irksome to me; it seems to threaten my liberty; every duty is unpleasant; every act of virtue costs an effort. Besides, I am, in myself, incapable of any supernatural work, and even of thinking of, or designing, any such. I continually need present grace, to inspire good actions, and help me in their performance.

In this state, which is that of my whole life, how can I think well of myself? of what can I boast? and concerning what can I not be grievously ashamed and confounded?

This is the self-knowledge imparted by faith, combined with the testimony of my own feelings and experience. The purest and healthiest of philosophies would never have taught me half so much. Man has ever been the chief object of the study and the consideration of sages. But the most glorious genius, with all its penetration and all its researches, can never learn self-knowledge; and, to my mind, that is an exceedingly humbling thing. If faith do not enlighten me, reason alone will never tell me that I came forth from nothing, and that GOD is my Creator; it never told any ancient sages that truth: they were all ignorant of this primary connection between man and GOD, which is the foundation of all the rest. And how strangely at a loss they were, in consequence of their ignorance respecting the origin of man! What marvellous absurdities they uttered on the subject! Our modern infidels have done very much the same.

As concerns tendency to evil, and repugnance to good, the inherent frailty of creatures, the nature of sin considered with regard to GOD, and the necessity of grace; the most religious philosophy had a faint glimmering on some points, and clear notions on none; but in most respects it was involved in thick darkness.

Then what did it know about the matter? What no one can ignore: the troubles of life, the weakness of childhood, the infirmity of age, the natural defects of body and mind, the passions, and their tyranny and disorder, the necessity of death, and, together with that, the uncertainty of a future state. This was a wretched, miserable sort of knowledge, and made most philosophers bitterly revile nature, and accuse her of treating us like an unjust stepmother. They were right enough, according to their lights; and the destiny of man must have appeared the more deplorable to them, because they could find no remedy for his troubles, either in their own vain systems, or in the false religion of the people.

Yet they were rather offended than humbled by this knowledge, painful as it was; because it really was too imperfect, and, though it could not fathom the depths of our misery, offered no counterpoise to that portion which it did perceive.

It is otherwise with our holy faith. Our religion makes man little in his own eyes, deeply humbles him, reduces him to nothingness, and less than nothingness, but at the same time supports and comforts him, and rouses hope, and shows him what great cause he has to trust in GOD. And indeed it also gives him a high idea of himself, for it unveils his true greatness, the nobleness of his faculties, his close connection with God, the sublimity of his destiny, the fatherly care of Providence, the inestimable benefit of redemption, and the price paid for his soul by GOD Incarnate. It even teaches him to reverence his body, as the temple of GOD, intended one day in glorious resurrection to share the eternal happiness of the soul.

This is the knowledge religion gives us concerning human nature; and this light is safe, for it is founded on infrangible revelation; it is bright and piercing, and perpetually increased by study and the practice of piety; it crushes down human pride, and elevates the soul with a Divine uplifting.

But, in addition to the motives for humility furnished by study of the Gospel, and practice of its precepts, GOD has many and many another way of humbling those whom He intends to attain a high pitch of holiness. He makes them feel that their light is darkness, and their will weakness; that their firmest resolutions are utterly frail, and that they are unable of themselves to amend the smallest fault or perform the slightest act of virtue. He allows them to feel great repugnance for their duties; their pious exercises are painful, and almost intolerable, because they are full of dryness, listlessness, and weariness; the passions they fancied were dead rise up again, and cause them strange conflicts; the devil tempts them in countless ways, and they seem given up to the wickedness and corruption of their own hearts; so that they see in themselves nothing but sin and great desire to sin. In the light of His infinite holiness He shows them the impurity of their motives and the selfishness of their aims, the stain of self-love on their good actions and its poison in their virtues. He calls to remembrance all their negligence, and cowardice, and faithlessness, and self-seeking, and desire of approbation and human respect; He brings them to hate and despise themselves for their ungrateful abuse of all His many graces.

For their yet greater self-abasement He appears to turn His face from them, and deprives them of all sensible gifts and graces, leaving them in miserable nakedness, from the sight of which they shrink, yet cannot close their eyes. He seems to be angry with them and to forsake them; and, on the other hand, He allows men to suspect their piety, to call it hypocrisy, to vex them with calumny and persecution; and this He suffers to happen not only on the part of wicked men and ordinary Christians, but also on that of virtuous persons of good understanding and exemplary life, who, while they decry and ill-treat these servants of GOD, fancy that they are honouring the Master. CHRIST JESUS, the Saint of saints, willed to bear all these miseries and contumelies, and greater yet than these; because He made Himself the Victim for sin: and upon His own beloved friends He bestows a precious draught from the same bitter cup. Thus, perfecting humility, He perfects sanctity, and sets them in a safe hiding-place against all temptation.

Then let us ascend and descend by this wondrous ladder of the knowledge of GOD and ourselves. We will mount as high and go down as low as, by the help of grace, we can; and when we have done all we can, we will pray that GOD may raise and abase us yet more, by means known only to Himself.

The more a soul really ascends, the less it is conscious of its ascent; and the further it descends the less it apprehends its descent. This seems a paradox; but it is most true. Advance in the knowledge of GOD increases the sense of unworthiness in the soul's feelings towards Him. In like manner, the deeper it sinks in self-knowledge, the more it is led to judge that it does not hate and despise itself enough. Thus it becomes exalted and humble, or, in other words, is an unconscious saint.

SECOND MAXIM.

Yield liberty to God, and have no will but His.

"*Into Thy hands I commend my spirit.*"

II.

OF CHRISTIAN LIBERTY, AND OF THE ACTIVE AND PASSIVE WAY.

In order to the better comprehension of what I have now to say, I think best to lay down, in the first place, certain incontrovertible principles.

At our creation GOD bestowed on us reason and understanding, in order that we might know and love Him; He purposed that we should eternally enjoy this love and knowledge, and also that such enjoyment should be our reward; therefore it became necessary that it should be deserved. To this end he placed us on earth for a certain space of time, known only to Himself. He gifted us with liberty; that is, with command over our actions, in order that, being performed by our own will, they might merit praise or blame, reward or punishment. Praise and reward are thus attached to the free fulfilment of the duties imposed on us by GOD; and blame and punishment follow the wilful violation of those duties.

Liberty, in its abstract, hath no essential power of doing good or ill; else GOD, who possesses supreme liberty, would not be free, because He can never will, or do, evil. Therefore our power of doing wrong does not proceed from our liberty, but from two other causes. The first of these is, that being necessarily dependent on God by a moral dependence, our actions ought to follow the rule of His will; so that they are morally good if they conform to it, and morally bad if they do not. The second is, that being defective in our very nature, it is possible that our conduct may swerve from this rule. From these two causes, combined with the free-will which simply makes us masters of our actions, arises that fatal power of sinning which it would be unjust and blasphemous to accuse God of having given us. It did indeed depend on Him to prevent its effect, but no reason obliged Him to do so; and His supreme wisdom judged fitter to permit that consequence, because it could not be prejudicial to His glory. Unquestionably, the most perfect liberty is that possessed by God, Who can will nothing but what is right. Therefore, the more our liberty resembles His, the nearer it approaches perfection; and the more unlike it is, the more imperfect it becomes. The will to sin is a defect and abuse of liberty, and the stronger and more habitual the will the greater the defect.

It is quite evident that we ought to desire never to abuse our liberty, but by our love of right and hatred of wrong, to bring it into the closest similarity with that of God. The greater our moral necessity of doing right, the more we shall be free like Him who hath this necessity in His nature; the greater our moral necessity of doing ill, the more our liberty will be fettered. Therefore S. Paul says that when the will yields to evil it becomes the servant of sin; and, on the other hand, that being free from sin, it is the servant of righteousness. Two opposite conditions: the first debases liberty; the second exalts and perfects it; for GOD Himself is, if we may so speak, the Servant of Righteousness, and infinitely more so than we can be, and in this servitude consists His perfect liberty. Thus also CHRIST said to the Jews: "He that committeth sin is the servant of sin;" and, "If the SON, therefore shall make you free, ye shall be free indeed."

But grace alone can deliver us from the bondage of sin, and give us real liberty; whence it follows that the more our wills subject themselves to grace, and the more they endeavour to depend fully and constantly upon it, the freer they will become. Their perfect deliverance is reserved for heaven, where they will once for all be established in holiness. But in this world, however thoroughly they may have submitted themselves to the dominion of grace, they are always liable to throw off the yoke, and must always be on their guard against that risk.

That risk will be the more or less imminent, according as the soul continues to be its own master, or gives itself freely up to be dealt with according as GOD wills. And so, all it has to do is to lay itself in His hands, to use its activity only in order to become more dependent on Him; to let grace act freely in all circumstances, and to its full extent, the soul reserving no power to itself except in order to thorough correspondence with grace.

These principles being laid down, it is clear that surrender of liberty is the same thing as devotion to GOD; because devotion is only an engagement to forsake self-will, and follow the will of God. This gift of liberty may be made in two ways, of which one depends on ourselves, and the other on God. It depends on ourselves, while retaining the exercise of liberty, to determine that it shall be subjected to the inspirations of grace, and to keep to this resolution. It depends on God to make Himself really Master of our liberty, by reason of our thus yielding it to Him; to govern it Himself, and, without doing it violence, to keep it captive in His hand. Hence arise two methods of serving God, one of which is called the Active, and the other the Passive way. Both are good; both are agreeable to God; both are interior; both adapted to make saints.

Following the first way, a Christian makes due use of the faculties bestowed on him by God—of memory, understanding, and will; he exercises them himself. Although directed by grace, and fully intending to follow its direction, he yet preserves his own liberty, and considers, judges, and chooses, concerning all things pertaining to his salvation. He meditates on the truths of the Gospel; by effort of his will he acquires love for them, he applies them to himself, and makes them the rule of his conduct. He forms resolutions, and endeavours to reduce them to practice; he uses pious methods, and holy ingenuities suggested by the Spirit of God, or by good books and the examples of the saints. Thus, by continual thought and perseverance, together with the assistance of prayer, advice, and sacraments, he succeeds in correcting his faulty habits and in acquiring Christian virtues.

Most of those who are seriously working out their salvation travel by this path, which is the most common, and is that taught by most popular books on devotion. This is the reason why we have so many methods, and exercises, and practices, for learning to meditate, or for hearing Mass, or for Confession, or Communion. And in this way it is always necessary to begin, except in peculiar cases; and it must always be persevered in, unless GOD Himself call us from it. Let this point be remembered; it is of the greatest importance, as it destroys illusions, and saps the foundations of Quietism.

We enter the passive way, when we feel ourselves drawn by a strong and sweet working of grace, which, in order to gain space for its action, leads us to suspend our own; when we are inwardly moved to yield up our heart and liberty and natural self-government completely and irrevocably into the hands of GOD. Thus GOD takes possession of the powers of the soul; acts upon them, and makes them act as He will; and man only follows, though yet freely, in the path marked out for him. He holds himself prepared to do at any moment what GOD may require of him; and GOD, by secret inspiration, does cause him to know what He requires; but yet this inspiration never involves disobedience to the Church, to rule, or to lawful authority; for there are no souls more docile or submissive than those which walk in this way.

Here, then, all exercise of natural liberty with regard to interior things (for of such only am I speaking) consists in seconding, and in never forestalling, Divine motions. As soon as they are resisted, or forestalled, the human spirit is plainly at work; but in the state of which we speak the Christian lies under the hand of GOD, like an instrument on which and by means of which He works. Not, however, a purely passive instrument, but one which consents and co-operates by its own act, often with extreme repugnance, and with violence to itself. Its state may very well be compared to that of a child writing under its master's guiding hand.

Now it is easy to imagine why this way is called passive, and wherein it differs from the active way. In the latter, the powers of the soul, assisted by grace, work, as it were, of themselves, and by their own exertion. Like the child writing from his master's copy, under his inspection, and obedient to his teaching, the soul chooses a subject of reflection, applies its various powers to it, forms chains of reasoning, produces affections, examines, deliberates, considers what to do, weighs arguments, and comes to a determination. All this, as we see, is active.

The passive way is not without activity; but then the action of God gives impetus to ours. The soul remains freely attentive, supple, and docile to Divine motions, as the child freely submits its hand to that of its master, intending to follow all its movements. But in like manner as the child, though able to write, waits till the master shall guide its hand; so the powers of the soul, bound and suspended, only exert themselves on the object to which God applies them, and in such manner as He applies them. This work is then more simple, more intense, and therefore less perceptible; so that the soul often thinks it is doing nothing, while the case is really quite otherwise.

The soul is naturally active and restless; but when subdued by that Divine attraction which leads it to rest, it dwells in habitual calm. In prayer, no distinct object presents itself to the mind; it usually sees things in a general and indistinct manner. The sense of GOD's presence is a peaceful and permanent feeling, not ex-haled in express acts of affection. The heart is filled, without effort on its own part. The lips speak, the hand writes, of Divine things without premeditation: GOD Himself guides all: and the recollection of what has been said or written remains not with the agent. There is no study how to root out faults, or gain virtues by such and such particular means; but GOD, by His continual action on the soul, and the practices He requires of it, and the interior trials with which He visits it, insensibly purifies it from its faults, and impresses on it those various virtues which He makes it exercise on occasion, without its thinking of them, or even imagining itself in possession of them.

In this way there is more of what is infused, and, in the other, more of what is acquired; but yet in such a manner, that that which is infused is also in a certain sort acquired, because pains are needed to preserve and to increase it.

Here I am only speaking of the ordinary passive way, otherwise called the way of bare faith. The extraordinary way, which is very rare, is that in which are found ecstacies, revelations, visions, and other like favours; and in which the devil troubles body and mind with vexatious and divers torments. I shall say nothing about that, because it ought neither to be desired nor feared; nor is it right to indulge curiosity concerning it, nor to read books treating of it, except when necessary for the guidance of others.

Such, roughly stated, is the difference between the active and passive ways. All men may and ought to walk in the first, by the help of ordinary grace; it is for GOD alone to open the gate of the second. Yet it is true that by their own fault many souls either do not enter it, or cease to walk in it. It is also true, that, according to the intention of GOD, the first would very often dispose souls to the second, if they responded more faithfully to grace, and were more generous, and brave, and simple; and if they could make up their minds to get rid of their own self-will; and if the entrance were not barred by their many mistaken notions.

But as this way is far the most conducive to our sanctification, because GOD then undertakes it and works at it without medium, it is most important to put away all such notions, and to neglect nothing which may open it to us; for I am persuaded that GOD calls more souls thereunto than is supposed. The necessary point is to recognise the marks of such calling, and to obey it with docility.

Some persons are invited to it by an inward attraction, from their earliest years; the proof of this is to be found in the lives of many Saints. If this attraction were followed, if good parents and instructors of youth, instead of discouraging it, would favour it and carefully put aside all things adverse to it; if confessors would take pains to cultivate the first seeds of grace, and to develop this germ of interior life; the number of souls led by the SPIRIT of GOD would be infinitely greater, especially among women, whose quiet education, and natural disposition, render them better adapted for Divine operations. The innocence of childhood, when the soul is simple, teachable, and unprejudiced, is unquestionably most favourable to perfect devotion; and if children were early guided in that direction, by lessons suited to their age, and with the necessary tact, skill, and patience, wonderful fruits would afterwards result from such education.

Others, later in life, after walking for a longer or shorter time in the common way, find that they can no longer fix their mind on meditation, nor even produce the same affections as heretofore; they feel distaste for the methods which they have hitherto followed. Something inexplicable leads them to suspend all action in their prayer: God Himself induces them to this, by giving them the enjoyment of most sweet peace and calm. When this state is not temporary, but continues in spite of repeated endeavours to pursue the former road, it is an infallible mark that God wills to take possession of such souls, and bring them into the passive way.

Others are prepared for it by distress, agitation, temptation, and dejection, which they can neither understand nor express. God, purposing to raise a new building in their hearts, shakes the former one, breaks it down, and destroys it to the foundation. It is the work of an experienced confessor to discover God's design herein, and to persuade those who are in this critical state to make full sacrifice of self, and to yield themselves thoroughly to His will. This sacrifice being made, agitation ceases, the soul feels a peace hitherto unknown, and enters a new region.

There are some persons who, though leading pious lives, are dissatisfied with themselves and with their own state, and feel that God requires some other thing of them, and seek they know not what. An opportunity furnished by Providence at last leads them to some person who, though unacquainted with them, and without very well knowing why, speaks to them at once of the interior life. Immediately their uneasiness ceases, and they are tranquillized and satisfied when least expecting it; for they have found that which they had long been seeking.

Not only righteous men, but sinners, and great sinners too, are called by GOD into the passive way. Some, at the moment of their conversion, are suddenly transformed by grace, and become new creatures, like S. Mary Magdalene, S. Paul, S. Mary Ægyptiaca, and S. Augustine. Others, after spending many years in exercises of penitence, are raised gradually to a state of sublime contemplation. It is difficult to believe, and yet is perfectly true, that the sudden and wonderful change wrought by Divine mercy in sinners, is usually more perfect and solid than that wrought in the righteous. Full of the sense of their own wretchedness and of GOD's wonderful goodness, they give themselves to Him more generously, are more deeply humbled by His favours, and bear His purifying trials more bravely.

But all, whether righteous men or sinners, who have walked in the passive way, entered it in no other manner than by giving up their liberty to GOD entirely and absolutely; saying, like S. Paul, "'LORD, what wilt Thou have me to do?' I am no longer mine, but Thine." They could enter it no otherwise; for GOD only takes what is given Him; the violence He does to the soul at that time is always gentle, and He waits the consent of the heart whereof He wills to be Master.

And what cause is there for fear in thus

yielding ourselves to GOD? His tender invitations, His earnest solicitations, have no other object but our good, our real good, which He understands infinitely better than we do, which He desires more keenly, and which He only can procure. Is not our salvation incomparably safer in His hands than in our own? If we unreservedly trust Him with our dearest interests, do we not preserve them from all those dangers to which the devil and our own hearts would expose them? Is any power strong enough to wrest our souls from GOD, after His acceptance of them, unless they themselves are cowardly and faithless enough to draw back? Can we more strongly induce GOD to take care of us than by surrendering ourselves to Him?

If we have any faith, or if we have one spark of love for GOD, if we have any wise love for ourselves: in whatever light we consider the matter, how can we hesitate?

I say, if we have any wise love for ourselves. For what is such love? It is the desire and endeavour to obtain our most perfect welfare. Therefore it is the love of GOD, and His glory: and of His interests, with which our own are closely interwoven. There is no doubt that we shall love ourselves in heaven. But how? Just as we shall love GOD: we shall be unable to associate any differing love with that. If we could form a distinct act of love for self, we should immediately fall from beatitude.

It may be objected that the passive way is not open to any and every person who wishes to walk in it, and that I myself have averred that none must enter it till GOD calls them. All this I grant. But I say that there are certain states of mind which prepare us for such a call, and that these are in our power. And I say further that, even if this call never comes, we may have the merit of preparing for it.

The first thing to do is to conceive a real, quiet, patient wish for living under the power of grace, and to offer ourselves frequently to God, that He may vouchsafe to reign in our hearts. The second is to do all our good works with the view of obtaining this blessing. The third is to observe extreme fidelity to God, and strict correspondence to all His inspirations, according to our present state.

For this purpose the following prayer of S. Ignatius may be used:—

"Receive, O Lord, the whole freedom of myself. Accept my memory, my understanding, my entire will. Whatsoever I have or possess, Thou hast of Thy bounty bestowed it upon me. All this I restore to Thee, and surrender it to be disposed of absolutely according to Thy will. Only give me love for Thee, along with Thy grace, and I am rich enough; I ask for nothing more."

THIRD MAXIM.

Pray for a wise guide, whom, when thou hast found, trust, revere, and obey.

"*If there be a messenger with him, an interpreter, one among a thousand, to show unto man His uprightness, then He is gracious unto him.*"

III.

OF GOOD DIRECTION.

THE chief reason which should lead a Christian to devote himself to GOD is, that He is the great, and, strictly speaking, the only Director of souls. CHRIST is not only the Way, which He points out to us by His doctrine and example: He is also the inward Guide; He is the Shepherd Who gives good pasture, and, by secret motions and inspirations, leads His sheep to find it. Nevertheless, according to the order of His Providence, He makes use of the ministry of priests for the direction of souls; on that ministry He bestows His grace, and through it He gives advice and instruction. He is ever the Master: He and He only can speak to the heart. But He speaks to it especially when His ministers, in the exercise of their functions, speak to the outward ear; He wills that they be heard and obeyed, as His representatives.

Therefore every one who aspires to Christian perfection, if he be free to choose a director, ought to seek of GOD, that he may be rightly guided in his choice. And this will certainly be granted if the prayer is made in real faith.

There is no point concerning which we are more easily blinded, or more apt to be prejudiced. Therefore we ought to lay the matter in GOD'S hands, simply and honestly resolving to take the person He points out, in spite of prejudice, or aversion, or any human feeling whatever.

The same thing must be done when there is good reason for changing a director. Such a change is right and desirable in certain cases; as, when he is unskilful, or careless, or wanting in firmness or gentleness, or unspiritual in his leading, etc. Then, having thoroughly weighed the matter in the presence of GOD, we must act firmly and put aside all unnecessary considerations.

And the choice is the more difficult, because good directors are extremely rare, and the external marks whereby to recognise them are very defective. Think of the combination of qualities which go to form a perfect director. He should be a man of an interior spirit, experienced in heavenly things, perfectly dead to self, closely bound to GOD, devoid of self-will, desiring neither to rule nor enslave the soul he leads; seeking in nothing his own glory and interests, but in all things the interests and glory of GOD; susceptible of no attachment save that inspired by charity; exercising his ministry with perfect independence; above all method and system, infinitely pliable to the inspirations of grace; able to assume different attitudes in order to meet the different needs of souls, and GOD'S designs regarding them; wise with Divine wisdom, gentle without softness, compassionate without weakness, firm without rigidity, zealous without hastiness; making himself all things to all men; condescending, in a certain degree, to human misery, prejudice and weakness; perfectly calm and patient; reproving, consoling, urging, checking, yielding, or resisting, according to circumstances; sustaining, encouraging, humbling, showing the soul its own progress, or else concealing it, as may be most needful. In fact, he ought to be a man who does nothing of himself in the matter of direction, but who seconds the work of GOD, without either hurrying or slackening it; following grace step by step, proceeding exactly as far as, and no further than, it leads. Are such men common amongst us?

Then we cannot too earnestly pray GOD that He would find us a director of this kind; for it is one of the greatest graces He can bestow, and one which may be the source of all others. Used aright, it will surely lead us to perfection. Would it not be intolerably presumptuous to fancy we could make such a choice by our own discernment; and would it not be most dangerous to look upon it in any but the highest light?

I am well aware that all persons cannot choose their own confessor, and that those who decide the matter for us often do not follow out the will of GOD. And it is undoubtedly an evil to fall, consciously or not, into the hands of an ill-qualified director. But then GOD supplies what is lacking in His minister; He takes upon Himself to lead us in His ways; and He will never fail us, if we are faithful to Him. So He directed Paul and Mary Ægyptiaca in the desert; so, in heathen countries He directs Christian souls destitute of almost all external help. So, in country places, where priests are careless or ignorant, the HOLY GHOST is the immediate guide of honest souls, and teaches them the secrets of the interior life.

However, we must not fail to give our thorough confidence to a man whom we may reasonably believe Providence to have sent us; when we feel that his words lighten our darkness, scatter our doubts, wake us from languor, warm our heart, and lead us to serve GOD more worthily; when we feel by experience that such a man is the instrument of GOD, really aiding the secret operations of grace; and especially if he leads us in the the way of recollection, prayer, and interior mortification; for that is the touchstone of true direction.

Generally, GOD inspires us with the will to begin by making a general confession, so as to inform the priest, not only of our past faults, but of the graces we have received, the dangers from which we have been shielded, the inward drawings which we have neglected or obeyed, the vices and temptations to which we have been most subject. Thus he becomes acquainted with our whole life, our disposition, the usual state of our soul, the various attempts of grace upon us, the obstacles which stop us, the exact point at which we stand: he is better able to see what GOD expects from us, and how he is to co-operate with His designs.

Through the whole course of direction, nothing ought to be kept hidden, whether as to the lights given us by GOD, or the desires and aversions of nature, or the suggestions of Satan, whose sleights and artifices we cannot unravel without aid. Anything which secret pride, or temptation of the devil leads us to hide or disguise, is sure to be the point which it is most important we should mention; and, however humiliating, it must never be kept back.

Also it is necessary to be on our guard against suspicions, prejudices, and fancies which cross the mind, or which the devil injects in order to diminish the trust we place in our director. For this is Satan's great object; and as soon as he sees that a director is working hard for our spiritual improvement, he seldom fails to inspire us with feelings of distrust and alienation. We cannot be too much on the watch against this danger. Almost always the evils arise from allowing ourselves to criticise the manner of our direction. "Why did he forbid me that? Why did he treat me in this way?" Then we argue, and judge, and censure; confidence is shaken, obedience fails; we lose sight of God, and look only at man.

Here I may remark, that one of the most certain signs of a disposition to the interior life, is that candour and lovely openness which leads the soul to disguise nothing, as to defects, or faults, or motives; to make no excuses; plainly to speak out on subjects which may humiliate it, and may lessen the good opinion of others. How rare, and how precious in the sight of God is this humble ingenuousness!

But it is not enough to be open with our confessor; we must hear his advice and his decision reverently, as if they issued from the lips of God. There must be no arguing with him, nor must we even mentally dispute anything contrary to our own ideas. In things touching the conscience, we must submit our way of thinking to his; believe the good and evil which he tells us of ourselves; justify nothing he condemns, nor, by false humility, blame what he approves. We pretend that we did not express ourselves properly, that he does not know us, that he does not see what passes within as well as we do; but these are poor pretexts, through which we assume the right of private judgment. The confessor judges more rightly of us, than we do of ourselves; let us hide nothing knowingly; and then, let our minds be at rest.

We know very well that we are blind as to what concerns ourselves, and that GOD wills to lead us by the way of faith and obedience. We act in a manner directly contrary to His intention, and make ourselves not only our own judges, but judges of our leaders. The devil tries to ruin us, through presumption or despair, by representing us to ourselves, as better or worse than we really are. These indocile and unsubmissive judgments of self are always dictated by self-love: they lead the conscience into error and blindness: are the beginning of scruples, anxieties, and all the sufferings of the imagination: they expose the soul to the most subtle snares of Satan and the most dangerous illusions.

The spiritual life has its dangers, and great dangers too, if it be misunderstood; and erroneous ideas concerning it are not uncommon. This evil must inevitably befal any one who professes to judge concerning himself of the workings of GOD or of Satan, and to distinguish by his own lights as to what proceeds from nature or from grace. Therefore, when we have clearly and honestly set forth our internal state, we must submit humbly and quietly, to the decision of the director. If he were mistaken, which might be the case, for he is not infallible, no harm would accrue to us from his error; GOD would yet bless our submission and obedience; He would hinder or repair the effects of the mistake. He has bound

Himself to do so by His Providence, because it is His will that we should see Himself in the minister who fills His place. This principle is the sure foundation, and only basis of spiritual direction.

I allow that it requires great faith always to behold God in a man who, after all, is subject to error, and not exempt from faults; it is no little sacrifice to give up our own ideas and conviction, in the very matters which interest us most deeply. But without this sacrifice, there can be no obedience of the judgment, and without such obedience, there is no real direction.

In the last place, we must punctually and faithfully perform all the director bids us do; and if through weakness, or indolence, or for any other reason, we have failed, we must tell him so. By this faithfulness alone we can advance. He will often prescribe things very painful to nature; practices which will humble us in the eyes of our neighbour; practices of continual subjection, sometimes so apparently petty and minute, that our pride will disdain them; practices opposed to our minds, our tempers, our dearest inclinations; and if he has the spirit of God, he must act thus, because the aim of God is our mortification. We must be determined to obey him in all things wherein we do not perceive manifest sin; and if we think it right to offer any remonstrance, it must always be subject to his decision.

It would be wrong to put before him such difficulties and impossibilities, as are frequently imaginary, and are the effect of strong prejudice or temptation. At any rate, after alleging them, if he pays no attention to them, we must yield, and resolve to obey. This will be easier than it seems. Nothing is impossible to grace and obedience; and if the victory over self require great efforts, it will be all the more glorious and meritorious. Virtues are God's gifts; He almost invariably grants them as the reward of some signal effort, after which the things previously found most difficult become easy. Innumerable proofs of this are to be seen in the lives of the Saints.

[Subjoined are a few notes from the "Priest's Prayer Book," which may meet some of those many cases in which the conditions of true direction do not exist, and may also guard against mistaken apprehension of some passages in the foregoing chapter.

"The object of direction is to form Jesus Christ in the soul (Gal. iv. 19), and especially to give a religious tone to secular life.

"Direction, therefore, is guidance in questions of practical action, afforded to Christians in doubt or difficulty, by one who is wiser in spiritual matters than they.

"Therefore, unlike the Sacramental rites of the Church, the efficacy of direction depends on the personal character and abilities of the director."

For example of the fallible character of direction on the part of a divinely appointed confessor, cf. 2 Sam. xii. 13, and 2 Sam. vii. 1-5.

"A director should confine himself to general guidance, and enter as little as possible into minute details. He should endeavour rather to instil maxims and principles, than to construct a code of minute observances.

"The director should aim at strengthening the sense of personal responsibility in those who consult him, and at increasing the sensitiveness and vigour of their consciences.

"The director should therefore reserve his aid for matters of real difficulty. If applied to in simple and obvious cases he should rather, by appealing to the conscience of the inquirer, endeavour to draw the answer from his lips.

"A constant change of directors is inadvisable; but there are two cases in which it is desirable to sever the connection between guide and pupil. (1) When constraint has grown up between them, and they are no longer on a footing of mutual confidence. (2) When the pupil exhibits too blind and slavish a compliance with the suggestions of the director, and appears to be substituting his dictates for the operation of conscience."]

FOURTH MAXIM.

Be always mindful of the God who is present everywhere, and dwelleth in the heart of the righteous.

" *Walk before Me, and be thou perfect.*"

IV.

OF THE PRACTICE OF THE PRESENCE OF GOD.

NO spiritual exercise is more frequently recommended than that of the Presence of GOD; none is more useful, or more profitable for advancement in virtue; in fact, it is indispensable. How can you grow holy, and attain to union with GOD, if you do not habitually think of His Presence?—It is most efficacious. If GOD is always before your eyes, how can you help trying to please Him in all you do, and to avoid displeasing Him?—It is most simple; and, in its simplicity, it embraces all other means of sanctification. GOD, present with the soul, points out its duties from one moment to another.—It is most sweet. What can be dearer than the continual remembrance of GOD? what can be sweeter to one who desires to love Him and to be wholly His?—Lastly, it is a practice which the willing soul cannot find otherwise than easy.

GOD spake to Abraham, saying, " Walk before Me, and be thou perfect." He made mention of that one point only, because it contains all. David says of himself, that he had set GOD always before him. Why? " For Hé is on my right hand, therefore I shall not fall." If he had continued faithful to his rule, the sight of a woman would not have led him to adultery, and from adultery to homicide. All Saints, both of the old and new covenant, have had this practice greatly at heart; but this I need not remark, for it is well known: nor need I dwell on the advantages resulting from it, because they are evident to all. I shall confine myself to two points; first, the explanation of what is meant by walking in the presence of GOD; second, the indication of means to be employed for that purpose.

The Presence of GOD may be considered from different points. GOD is present to all things by His immensity. This presence is necessary, and extends to the just and unjust, the lost and blessed, and all creatures animate and inanimate.

GOD is also present to all things by His providence. He sees all things; not only actions, but most secret thoughts. He sees good, approves and rewards it; He sees evil, condemns and punishes it; rules all, directs all, according to His eternal designs; and, in spite of obstacles, makes all things work together for His glory.

GOD is present within the righteous in a special manner, by sanctifying grace. The heart of the righteous is His abode, saith S. Gregory the Pope. This is a presence of goodwill, charity, and union: this is the beginning of our merits; this makes us children of GOD, pleasing in His sight, and worthy of possessing Him hereafter for ever. It is communicated by baptism and restored by penance; it is habitual, and continues as long as we preserve the grace to which it is attached. Although no righteous man can answer for this presence of GOD within him, because no one knows whether he is worthy of love or hate, yet, when he has fulfilled the rules laid down for procuring it, he may reasonably believe that GOD has graciously bestowed it on him, and he must do all that in him lies to retain it.

GOD is present to the soul by actual grace, which enlightens the mind and attaches the will. This presence has its intervals; for, although grace is always offered to us, it does not always act, because its action presupposes certain dispositions on our part. This presence acts more or less on sinners; inspiring them with a sense of sin, and calling them to repent. Some are ceaselessly pursued by it; they cannot allow themselves a moment for thought, without hearing the voice of GOD, bidding them turn from their evil ways. Much more does it act upon the righteous, to turn them from evil, and excite them to holiness, and sanctify all their works. It is the more felt, and the more efficacious, according as attention and fidelity are more or less perfect.

Lastly, there is a presence of GOD, which consists of an habitual infused peace. This presence first makes itself known by its sweetness, which as S. Paul bears witness, passeth all understanding. Afterwards, it is only perceived, without being strongly felt, and at last, it is enjoyed, like health, without being noticed. GOD does not thus bless with His presence all righteous persons, but only those of whom He takes special possession, and whom He desires to place in the passive state. Others only experience its transitory effects.

The different kinds of presence being thus explained, it is easy to understand what is meant by walking in the presence of GOD. It is not merely the thought of GOD, such as may be entertained by a philosopher or a theologian, meditating on Divine things, without any reference to himself; but it is the thought of GOD, as connected with our habits and our conduct; it is the deduction from that thought of moral consequences and a rule of life. So that, in the exercise of the presence of GOD, a straightforward and pious will must direct the understanding, and the heart must have the chief share in the whole matter.

It is an error to suppose that this practice consists in violent efforts of the mind, striving to think in GOD continually. That is impracticable, even in perfect solitude and entire detachment from earthly things; much more in the case of persons living in the world, distracted by the necessities of life, by business, family worries, and other like matters. Shall it be said that such persons are not required to apply themselves to the practice of the presence of GOD? This would be true indeed, if, in order to feel GOD present with us, we must banish every other thought. But such is not the case; no Christian is exempt from this exercise on account of his condition; indeed, it is compatible with the most busy and active state of life.

He walks in the presence of GOD, who, when he can arrange his own time, uses regular exercises to recal him to GOD at different hours of the day: such as meditation, attendance on public means of grace, devotional reading, and vocal prayers; and who, as in the sight of GOD, employs himself well and usefully, avoiding idleness, and curbing his imagination.

He walks therein, who, when the day is filled up by necessary work (except morning and evening prayer, from which nothing can excuse a Christian), offers his principal actions to GOD, blesses Him before and after meat, thinks of Him from time to time, and frequently uses ejaculatory prayer.

He walks therein, who, like Job, takes heed to all his ways, watches his thoughts, and words, and works, in order to say and do nothing to wound his conscience and displease GOD. This practice is no constraint for one who fears GOD; still less for one who loves Him; and it is thus that all good Christians act. It is nothing but a faithful preservation of sanctifying grace and of GOD's favour; which is the primary duty of every Christian.

He walks therein more entirely who, like David, keeps the issues of his heart, in order always to hearken what the LORD shall speak to him, and the secret warnings He may give him: who studies to correspond to every inspiration of the HOLY SPIRIT, and to perform every action under the rule of grace. All interior persons follow this method, which is the fittest for leading them to perfection.

He, lastly, walks therein still more perfectly who, having been favoured with the infused peace of which I have already spoken, diligently endeavours not to part from it, dwelling always, as it were, within his own heart, in order to realize it; carefully putting aside all that endangers its loss, and eagerly embracing all that may preserve and increase it. This peace, as I have said, is purely the gift of GOD: it does not depend on ourselves whether we obtain it, but it is in our power, having obtained it, to preserve it.

As to the means which facilitate the exercise of the presence of GOD, some are general and some are particular.

The chief thing necessary is the removal of obstacles. When they are once out of the way, the presence of GOD becomes familiar to us, and as free, and, so to speak, as easy as the act of breathing. We must therefore mortify the desire of seeing, hearing, and knowing things which are useless or which do not concern us, and, in fact, all that pertains to curiosity; for curiosity draws us out of ourselves and casts us among external things, and the presence of GOD calls the soul to dwell within. We must put a stop to that natural restlessness which induces coming and going, and change of place, or object, or situation. This restlessness is really the effects of the uneasiness which overpowers the soul when it looks within itself and does not find GOD present. We must moderate eagerness and vehemence in our desires.

It is also necessary to curb the imagination, and gradually accustom it to quietness. If it escapes in spite of our endeavours, it must be brought back gently; we must take from it that whereon it feeds, such as vain shows, exciting books, and too great application to imaginative arts. Nothing is more dangerous than to give imagination too much of its own way, and nothing is more incompatible with the exercise of the presence of GOD. It is true that we are not wholly masters of that faculty, whose wanderings form the torment of pious souls; this is a great matter for humiliation and a fertile source of scruple for those who are not able to despise them. But this is in our power: to refuse it those objects which it ardently desires, and to which it furiously clings. Be careful to maintain great freedom of heart and mind, not allowing the thoughts to dwell continually on the past or on the future, but rather on the present, which alone is at your disposal. Put aside all useless thoughts, for it is equally contrary to the presence of GOD to think too much or too little. Do not meddle with other people's business. Set your own affairs in order, without over-much anxiety as to the result; be reasonably careful about them, and leave the rest to Providence. Take not too much business upon you, and keep spare moments for breathing time and for recollection. It is right to do good to others, and to attend to works of mercy, but these things have their measure, and cease to be right when they injure the soul. So much for liberty of mind.

As to liberty of heart, let nothing enter therein which shall affect it too sensibly, and agitate or vex it, exciting excessive desire or fear, joy or grief: nothing in fact which may enchain it or lead it away captive, or turn it aside from its one true object. As this exercise is one of love, the distraction of the heart is far more hurtful to it than that of the mind.

The greater the freedom of the mind and heart, the greater will be the facility of dwelling in GOD's presence, because GOD is always the first object that offers itself to either, when it is emptied of all things else.

The particular means to this end are, the frequent sight of such things as may remind us of GOD; as, the crucifix, religious prints or pictures, texts from Scripture or the Fathers; the use of the sign of the cross, (according to the custom of the first Christians, who, as Tertullian says, were accustomed to begin their most trivial actions by making that sign,) and the frequent use of aspirations drawn from the psalms or other Scriptures. If a little strictness be maintained at first, these habits will become pleasant and easy. If daily meditation is practised, the most striking thought or the deepest affections may be retained in the mind through the day. Every one may choose his own method in these matters, and follow or change it according to the benefit he derives from it.

But the chief means of acquiring the practice of the habitual presence of GOD, is the thought of CHRIST and His mysteries, and especially of His Passion. I shall speak of this more at length in the following chapter.

As to persons in the passive state, there is no need to teach them any particular method for dwelling in the presence of GOD. The HOLY SPIRIT leads them to the use of all due methods: they have only to yield themselves to His guidance. At their first entrance into the passive way, they feel too much happiness in their secret intercourse with GOD, to be tempted to allow themselves in anything that might interrupt it.

But afterwards, when they are deprived of sensible feeling, and GOD drives them, in some sort, out of themselves, to prevent them from noticing His work within them, they must beware of seeking from any creature those consolations which they no longer find in GOD. They would be punished with jealous severity; and if they persisted in such unfaithfulness, it would infallibly be followed by the loss of their position. Therefore, without subjecting themselves to any stated practice, let them be faithful to those which grace inspires; laying aside, of their own will, no pious exercise, labouring ceaselessly in external and internal mortification; and believing that, as GOD gives more to them than to others, so He will require more at their hands.

The habit of the presence of GOD is like all other habits. Difficult to acquire, but, once learned, easy and pleasant to retain. The sweet thought of GOD makes all other thoughts insipid. As the soul advances, it more clearly sees GOD in all things. The sight of things created recalls the thought of their Author, and the perfection of His works fills the soul with delight. In every event that takes place, whether in the world or the Church, whether temporal or spiritual, great or small, adverse or prosperous, the faithful soul perceives her LORD. Abiding closely at His side, her glory, her interests, her will are one with His. For her, time fades to nothingness, and eternity begins already. Such are the effects of the exercise of the presence of GOD.

FIFTH MAXIM.

Keep close to our Lord, and draw true love from its true source.

"*No man cometh to the Father, but by Me.*"

V.

OF DEVOTION TO OUR LORD.

CHRIST is the centre, not only of our religion, but of our spiritual life. In whatever path the soul may be led, active, passive, ordinary, or extraordinary, He is its One Guide and Pattern; the chief subject of its meditation and contemplation, the object of its affection, the goal of its course. He is its Physician, Shepherd, and King; its Food and Delight. And there is none other Name given under heaven, whereby men may be saved, or may come to perfection.

Therefore it is absurd and impious to fancy that there can be any prayer, from which the humanity of CHRIST is and ought to be excluded, as an object not sufficiently sublime. Such an idea can be nothing but an illusion of the devil. Contemplate the perfections of GOD, if you are drawn to do so: lose yourself, if you will, in the Divine Essence: nothing is more allowable or more praiseworthy, provided grace gives wings to the flight, and humility is the companion of that sublime contemplation. But never fancy that it is a lower course to look and gaze upon the SAVIOUR, whenever He presents Himself to your mind. Such an error is the effect of false spirituality and refined pride; and, believe it who will, leads directly to disorders of the flesh, by which GOD almost invariably punishes proud upliftings of the mind.

Know then that, as long as the soul has free use of its faculties, she must turn chiefly to CHRIST JESUS, whether in meditation or simple contemplation. That contemplation in which the understanding alone is exercised upon an entirely spiritual object, is too high for weak minds like ours, encumbered with a weight of flesh, and subjected in many ways to material things. So that, with some persons, it is less a prayer than a Platonic speculation; with others, a hollow imagination, in which they lose sight both of GOD and of themselves.

Besides, this contemplation is too bare and dry for the heart; it finds no food therein. The abstract consideration of infinite perfections contains nothing that excites to virtue, or that encourages in trouble. The repose obtained by this supposed prayer is false, and is a dangerous quietism. It leaves the soul dry, cold, full of self-esteem, disdain of others, distaste and contempt for vocal prayer (which our weakness greatly needs); for the common practices of piety, charity, and humility; and indifferent even to the most august and holy of our Sacraments.

If the powers of the soul are bound at the time of prayer, I can understand that it is then unable to think of CHRIST, or of any other subject. GOD, desiring to humble the mind, to destroy natural activity, and remove from the heart its immoderate love of sensible consolations, sometimes leaves the soul for many years in a void, wherein neither CHRIST, nor any other distinct object, is set before it.

However, in the first place, this is not the act of the soul itself, but a sort of martyrdom in which it acquiesces, because such is GOD's will. And when, during that fearful nudity, CHRIST is occasionally restored to it, with what joy it receives Him, and converses with Him during the brief moments of His stay!

> "How happy when I find at last,
> How joyous when I hold Him fast!"

In the second place, the soul thus treated endeavours to make up during the day for the loss from which it suffers in the time of prayer. It thirsts to be joined in Holy Communion to Him Who, in these seasons of dearth, is its only stay, its only food. It spends itself in holy ejaculations. It invents divers practices whereby to invoke and adore Him throughout the day in His various mysteries. It seeks Him in all spiritual reading, in all visits to His holy House; it turns to Him for all grace, and in all tribulation. There is no soul really and truly interior, whether passive or not, but strives to live in, and by, and for CHRIST.

How could it be otherwise? GOD the FATHER gave Him to us for this very end; He became man in order to unite us with Himself. Sin had parted GOD and man too widely. CHRIST assumed our nature in order to do away with that separation. No man cometh to the FATHER but by Him; no man abideth in the FATHER but by Him.

S. Paul was not only an interior man, but was in the passive state, bound by the HOLY GHOST, and that to a wonderful degree. Yet his epistles are full of CHRIST.

S. John lay mystically on JESUS' bosom during his whole life, as he literally did at the Last Supper. But who ever reached a higher state of contemplation?

Ye who aspire to the interior life, that is, to a life of real piety, enter into CHRIST, as the author of the Imitation advises; study to know Him well; make this knowledge the usual subject of your meditation, and reading, and reflection; let everything have reference to it. Never fancy that you have exhausted, or even fathomed it.

Nor let it be enough to study CHRIST; lift up your hearts to love Him. The love of GOD and of GOD made Man are one and the same. Let this be the object of all your exercises. "If any man love not the LORD JESUS CHRIST, let him be anathema." He who loves Him faintly, is but an imperfect Christian; the true Christian longs and strives to love Him more and more, knowing that He can never be loved according to His due.

But love without imitation, would be vain and sterile. Therefore, be imitators of CHRIST. He is a perfect model, perfect in every feature. A model for all states and conditions. To all men, in all conceivable circumstances, CHRIST, in His mysteries, and virtues, and doctrine, gives lessons and examples. And, by His grace and Sacraments, He gives ample means for carrying them out.

But above all things meditate on His Passion; cling to His Passion; copy the example that you see in His Passion. Go to your prayers that you may draw love from His salutary Wounds, and especially from His pierced Heart. Remember that His Passion is the foundation of our whole religion; that the glorious Sacrifice of our Altars is but the memorial and renewal and extension of the Sacrifice of Calvary.

The Crucifix is, and always will be, the dearest book of pious souls; it speaks to the senses, to the mind, and to the heart; no other language is so eloquent and touching. It is within the understanding of the most simple and ignorant, and is, at the same time, above the comprehension of the greatest intellect and the utmost learning; it says all; it teaches all; it answers all; it excites to the greatest efforts; it consoles in the most bitter sorrows—nay, it changes their bitterness into sweetness.

Devout soul, do you desire to attain union with God, and the precious gift of His continual presence, making all labour light? Spend some time daily in prayer before the Crucifix; take no other subject of meditation; look at it, hold it in your hands, pray to Christ hanging on the Cross, that He would Himself be your Master and Director. Bid your mind be silent in His presence; let your heart only speak. Tenderly kiss His Hands and Feet; press your lips to the Wound of His Side; and your soul will be moved, and torrents of grace will flow into it, and with joy shall you draw water out of the wells of salvation; you will make progress in spiritual things, for the Cross contains them all.

And say not that the sight of the Crucifix does you no good, but leaves your heart cold and insensible; and that, however much you may try to express affection, you have no words wherewith to do so. If you cannot speak, you can listen. Stay silently and humbly at your Saviour's feet; if you persevere, He will not fail to instruct, and nourish, and strengthen you. And if you do not feel this at the time, you will perceive it gradually in your life. We are impatient, and want excited feelings; and therefore we leave off the most profitable practices, if they do not appear to succeed at once. Persevere, I say: you have greatly abused the love of CHRIST; let Him try yours a little; He will crown your perseverance, and your reward will be the gift of prayer.

SIXTH MAXIM.

Make good use of those two Sacraments whereof one brings cleansing and the other life.

"*Now ye are clean through the word that I have spoken unto you. Abide in Me and I in you.*"

VI.

OF THE SACRAMENTS OF PENANCE AND THE HOLY EUCHARIST.

WE all know that, after Baptism, which regenerates, but can only be supplied once, the two chief springs of grace are the Sacraments of Penance and the Holy Eucharist, which may be renewed as often as the soul stands in need of them. The former cleanses it from defilement, and renders it pure in GOD's sight; the latter maintains its spiritual life, by uniting it with the Very Author of that life. Therefore the right use of these two Sacraments greatly tends to sanctification; and his salvation is certain who does his best to receive them worthily, and profit by them fully.

It would lead me too far, were I to treat this matter at length, and my subject does not require it of me. I am not now writing for those who only go to Confession and to the Lord's Table, in order to obey the precept of the Church. This I will say, in case my book falls into their hands: as long as they do only so much as is absolutely of obligation, they run a great risk of not being rightly disposed for the reception of these

Sacraments; if they have any wicked habits, it is unlikely that they will be amended, as long as they receive good advice so seldom, and so seldom obtain the strength of the Blessed Eucharist: therefore their salvation is much imperilled.

Nor am I writing even for those who are used to confess and communicate on the great festivals only. Perhaps their lives may be exempt from glaring sins; but they are surely wanting in zeal for their own sanctification; and they neither respond to the desire of the Church, nor to our LORD's intention in His institution of the Sacraments. Let me advise them to read some good book on the advantages of frequent Confession and Communion; to obey the pressing invitation of the Church, and the advice of their confessor.

I write for those Christians only who, being resolved to lead a holy life, and knowing that frequent participation in the Sacraments is one of the most effectual means to holiness, have adopted the pious habit of confessing and communicating fortnightly, or weekly, or oftener, according as their occupations allow, and their confessor authorises. I also write for those dedicated to GOD, as Priests and Religious persons; who, by their rule, are obliged to frequent Celebrations or Communions.

And in addressing such persons only, I must deal with none but the most essential points; else I might fill volumes on the subject, even as many volumes have already been filled. But let me give this warning: be equally on your guard against books which set forth too lax ideas as to frequent reception, and those which frighten persons away from the Holy Table, by requiring such great perfection, as can only be the result of frequent Communion. And what I say of books, is also to be understood of confessors.

In the ancient Church Confession was rarer, and Communion more frequent. The Bishop was then the only, or almost the only, confessor; and if the primitive Christians, who communicated whenever they assisted at the Holy Sacrifice, (and in their own homes besides,) had confessed as often as devout people do now, the Bishop would have had no time to hear them. Their lives were holier than ours, and yet slight faults daily escaped them, which they did not think needful to bring to Confession. If they had aught against their brethren, they embraced each other, and were reconciled before offering their gifts; and as to venial sins, they believed, as S. Augustine teaches, that they were wholly effaced by the recitation of the LORD'S Prayer. Therefore they only applied to the Bishop, or his deputy, for sins of some little magnitude, or concerning which they stood in doubt; and we may believe that their consciences were at least as delicate as those of the devotees of the present day.

As time wore on, and the number of confessors increased, the facility of applying to them made Confession much more frequent; and the holy custom of communicating whenever present at Mass being lost, the idea took root that it was necessary to receive the advice or permission of the confessor: and this gave rise to regular weekly (or more frequent) Confessions.

Now, these continual Confessions, when made matter of obligation, are subject to abuse. They give rise to anxiety and scruples; the penitent worries himself to find something to say; dwells upon thoughts that he had better despise; and exposes himself to be wanting in contrition. Often there is no matter for Absolution, and yet it would be distressing if the confessor would give none. The worst is, that, without Confession, such persons will not go to Communion when they could and should do so. No one knows what it costs sensible confessors to bring some souls to reasonable practice in this matter; they take fright, and are scandalised; very often nothing can be done with them; and the confessor is fain to yield to their obstinacy.

Another abuse, still greater and more common, is that of believing that all perfection consists in frequent participation in the Sacraments. Many persons think themselves saints, because they communicate weekly, or daily, who yet never dream of correcting their faults; and who perhaps do not even know them, because they are so blinded by self-love; they are impatient, harsh, censorious, full of self-esteem and contempt of their neighbour, proud of the multitude of their external observances, and destitute of the slightest idea of internal mortification.

All the fruit they derive from their Communions and other pious exercises, consists in spiritual vanity, secret pride, and all the subtle vices engendered by devotion grafted on self-seeking.

A third abuse is that of treating Confession and Communion as matters of routine. Those who fall into this error, come to the Sacraments without any, or with superficial, examination, and because they are afraid of breaking their rule and attracting observation, or because the director has given such and such orders; and these most holy actions are performed in much the same way as the most ordinary business.

But consider each Sacrament apart. The thing most to be apprehended in the matter of frequent Confession is, that either the self-examination be insufficient, or else exaggerated and scrupulous. Persons of a giddy, thoughtless nature, and those whose devotion is cold and indifferent, are liable to examine themselves amiss. Some only consider their external actions, and scarcely give a thought to what passes within. Others have pet sins, of which they do not think at all. Others have a regular form of examination, which they say by heart to their confessor, generally in the same order and the same words. And there are some who, being habitually subject to venial sins—as, to breaking certain rules—and having no wish to correct them, leave them out of their examination and confession. In general, examination is ill performed, either from ignorance, or from want of watchfulness between the periods of confession, or from indifference to advancement in piety.

On the other hand, very timid souls, lively imaginations, and little minds, are apt to examine themselves too severely, or too anxiously: they see faults in everything; and these faults, which are sometimes none at all, are exaggerated and turned into monsters: they confuse thought with consent, and confound the first involuntary movement with the determinate act; they perplex themselves in their researches; hours are not enough for them; they go through torments every time they have to confess. This examination does not only weary them at the time of Confession, but all day long; they are perpetually searching into their conciences, and do nothing but fret and dissect themselves.

I grant that it is difficult to keep the happy medium between too much and too little. For those persons who lead a regular life, with few relations to the external world, and uniform occupations, and who make daily self-examination, I think that the scrutiny before Confession ought to take but little time: a glance should remind them of what they have done during the week. Persons otherwise circumstanced require more time, but such time has its limits: a quarter of an hour more than suffices for a weekly confession; and it is better to run the risk of forgetting some slight fault rather than put oneself to torture in order to omit none.

Examination should be made simply, quietly, and honestly, after having asked the HOLY GHOST for that light on which you ought to rely rather than on your own research. Do not make painful efforts of memory, but pray Him to show you those faults which most displease GOD, which offend your neighbour, which hinder your own progress; then think of those only which come into your mind. Pay more attention to habitual than to transitory faults, and to those which are in any way deliberate rather than to such as are simply inadvertent.

But it is more important to feel real contrition for sin, and make an earnest resolution of amendment. Such souls as I here have in view do not find this difficult as regards great sins, which I suppose they hold in habitual abhorrence. But that is not the case with respect to lesser sins of omission or commission connected with propensities which they treat tenderly, and against which they have not courage to fight resolutely; such as vanity, curiosity, laziness, self-indulgence, censoriousness, and so forth. The mention of these sins is repeated in every confession. It is very difficult to feel sincere contrition, or to resolve firmly not to commit them again, so long as the cause is allowed to subsist undisturbed. The branches merely are lopped off; but they grow again directly, because the root is spared. Contrition for venial faults, habitually and intentionally committed, is as suspicious as that for mortal sins of the same nature. Grace demands their correction; nature refuses it.

It is true that we can only attain to moral certainty of our contrition; but if there be any method of quieting our minds on that point, it is the formation of an earnest resolution to commit no fault intentionally or deliberately, and the acting on that resolution. Then nothing remains but faults of impulse, inadvertence, and of simple frailty, to which the will does but half consent. A determination to allow ourselves in no sins, readily wins from God the grace of repentance for those into which we do fall. Such repentance is not our own work: God grants it; and He only gives it to those who make good use of His other graces.

Doubt, O Christian soul, of the truth of your contrition, until you have fully made up your mind to eschew every voluntary sin. But, if you have done so, and live accordingly, then indulge in no more uneasiness about the matter. You must judge of your contrition, not by the feelings that you endeavour to excite at the time of Confession, nor by the acts that you then utter, but by your habitual hatred of sin, your degree of watchfulness against it, and your efforts to conquer evil propensities and habits. There is no rule but this; and this rule is safe.

You are alarmed sometimes, because you feel no grief, and your heart seems frozen, and your act of contrition appears to be a mere formal set of words. You used to feel really sorrowful: love constrained your heart, and you were even moved to tears. Look well into yourself: see if you do truly detest the sins you are going to confess. If so, be at ease, and seek no further certainty. Perhaps your state of mind is better than when you were touched with sensible grief. Therefore, dare boldly to cast aside all fears and doubts and scruples on this subject.

Besides, we do not excite contrition, as some suppose, by squeezing feelings out of our hearts, or moving ourselves to tears; but by humbly praying GOD Himself to inspire our souls with true repentance, and then simply and peacefully making an act of contrition.

Then comes the accusation, and it is often very defective—too much or too little detailed, by reason of self-love or false shame. As to the defects which result from ignorance, coarseness, or narrow-mindedness, the Confessor must remedy them by such questions as he shall see fit.

The accusation must be short and simple. No useless details, which often implicate other persons. No circumlocution. If you have to say that you were impatient, or wanting in charity, or so on, do not make a long story of it. Some people think they should make a bad confession if they did not repeat exactly all that was said to them, and all that they said in reply.

It must be clear and precise. No indistinctness, no ambiguity, no disguise. Let the confessor understand the thing as you understand it yourself. None of those vague accusations which merely occupy space and time. Those who wish to fill their confession with many subjects, are much given to the use of these. They accuse themselves of self-love and of pride: those are vicious habits, not sins. Or of slackness in GOD's service: the express point should be mentioned. Or of lukewarm Communion. What does that mean?

It must be thorough. No necessary circumstances suppressed. Together with the fault, mention the motive which induced it, and which is sometimes more sinful than the act itself. Do nothing in any way against your conscience. If any fault is particularly humiliating, or if you fear reproof for it, do not leave it to the end. Really humble souls always begin by naming such faults. It is also right to tell your temptations, and to explain wherein they consist, although you may have reason to believe that they have not been yielded to. Shame sometimes leads to the concealment of certain temptations; there is danger in this: it is a device of which the devil makes use in order to render a fall more easy, and it generally succeeds.

Lastly, the accusation must be exactly true. Faults are not to be exaggerated, diminished, nor excused. Call that certain which you believe to be certain; call that doubtful which you consider doubtful. Scrupulous and tempted persons are apt to say, that they have consented when they have not done so. The confessor should be on his guard, and not take them at their word: else he will cast them into despair. Some think that it is better to say more rather than less; they ought, if possible, to say neither more nor less. Persons of strong and lively imagination ought to mistrust it, when at Confession.

Early instruction on the subject of Confession is exceedingly important: because, at a certain age, it is almost impossible to correct the erroneous customs contracted by long habit.

Except in cases of violent temptation, etc., souls in the passive way examine themselves very quietly, and see the state of their conscience clearly; they neither become scrupulous, nor do they slur over anything, because GOD never fails to show them the least fault they commit; they are not uneasy about their contrition; they accuse themselves with childlike candour and simplicity. Their confessions are usually short, because they contain nothing needless. Unless obliged by rule, they only confess when necessary; when they do so under obligation, they simply state that they have nothing on their minds. By these signs, it is easy to know whether persons are in this way, or are disposed to enter it.

Some may ask, whether it is advisable to make use of those exercises for Confession and Communion, which are to be found in all manuals of devotion.

I consider them useful and necessary to those who seldom approach the Sacraments. They are fitted also for young people, who are trying to be good, and find great difficulty in collecting their thoughts. Acts, well repeated, inspire devotion where it previously did not exist; they either recall the mind or prevent it from wandering.

But I think that those who enjoy the blessing

of frequent Communion, ought to acquire the habit of dispensing with these helps; for, in the first place, familiarity diminishes their effect. In this respect particularly, novelty alone is striking. So that an exercise grows wearisome when it is known by heart, and leaves us cold and dry.

Another great objection is, that, when we find ready-made acts of virtues in our books, we do not excite our own hearts to produce them, but, having borrowed the feelings of the writers, we fancy that we have expressed our own. So these foreign feelings leave nothing behind them in our souls; while those which are born within us by the help of grace, feed and develop holiness, and produce that frame of mind, which, when frequently renewed, becomes a habit, and accustoms us to interior recollection.

Nor is it to be doubted that the expression of our own feelings is more agreeable to God, and belongs more truly to hearty devotion. What matter to Him all those regular methodical acts? The thoughts that please Him are those which He breathes into the soul; not those which the soul seeks elsewhere. If they are not necessary for the supply of our indigence and the fixing of our attention, we had better do without them, and leave our hearts at liberty to pour themselves out before God. Free and untutored feelings are more natural, more lively, and more effective.

Therefore I would have you try gradually to leave off using books, both before and after Communion. Let your preparation and thanksgiving be made quietly, without wearying your mind: and with the alone help of God, Who is never so near us as in the holiest of actions. And while acknowledging the insufficiency of your own attempts to receive CHRIST worthily, and worthily to thank Him for this inestimable benefit, I would wish you trustfully to ask Himself to dispose your heart aright; and then firmly believe and fully expect that He will do so, and remain quietly recollected; give Him full liberty over your heart, both as to preparation for His reception, and as to His taking entire possession of it.

This divine method, in which CHRIST would give us His fulness, and we should give Him simplicity, humility, faith, love, and trust, would be much better than our bustle and activity, and the shakings we give our souls in order to produce a little sensible fervour. Its effect would be perfect peace; a sweet suspension of the powers of the soul; a loving expectation of our LORD's coming: an unspeakable blessedness in His Presence. But self-love must always be busy, and so spoils everything. It seems to fear that GOD cannot do as well as it can itself; and therefore, wherever self-love interferes, GOD does little, or nothing.

For the last two hundred years there has been great searching out of methods for hearing Mass well, and communicating devoutly. They will never be found, so long as they are sought only in books. The true method ought to be in our hearts; and books are useful only while they help to implant it in them. Because we begin by using a prayer-book, are we therefore never to learn to do without it? The following is the best method I know, and I deduce it from the very nature of the Eucharist:—

Consider it as a Sacrifice, wherein CHRIST offers Himself to His Father, and offers us together with Himself. Hereby He plainly intimates that we have only to unite ourselves to

His oblation, and to make it with the same intentions and dispositions as He Himself does. We know what these are. Let us make them our own, not by a multiplicity of distinct acts, but by one act very simple and intense. Let us pray Him to instil them into us; then let us keep ourselves in a state of recollection, and leave to His grace the care of occupying our minds during the celebration of the Holy Mysteries. All He requires is that we should not bring with us profane or idle thoughts, nor allow ourselves in distractions, and, that, as far as possible, we should keep our hearts quiet and our minds attentive. He will take charge of the rest, if we trust to Him. I know by experience that if, at the beginning of Mass, we said simply and earnestly: "LORD, cause me to assist at Thy holy Sacrifice in a manner worthy of Thee: I cannot do so of myself:" we should feel the effects of our faith and humility: CHRIST would act upon our souls, and would keep them in a reverent and loving silence; and we should rise from our knees with an impression of grace upon us which it would be easy, with due watchfulness, to retain throughout the day.

Consider the Eucharist as a Sacrament, wherein CHRIST gives Himself to us with the full affection of His heart. Let us give ourselves to Him as thoroughly and as sincerely. He longs to unite Himself to us; let us long in like manner to unite ourselves to Him. His delights are to be with the sons of men; let us delight in possessing Him. This must be our habitual state of mind: not necessarily expressed in many words. If this be not our condition, let us pray simply and quietly that it may become so, and endeavour to remove all things within us that are opposed to such a state. We should be humbled and ashamed at being so cold and indifferent. Such should be our remote and daily preparation for Communion: it is certainly the essential point.

As to the proximate preparation, let it be a prayer to our LORD that He would prepare us Himself. Will He not do it better than we can, with all our methods and exercises? Why not ask Him? As to our thanksgiving, we should leave Him to act within us as He pleases. If He desires acts, He is fully able to suggest them. I see no other to be made on our part than to worship and love Him from the bottom of our hearts, without saying anything to Him. But we want to act and to feel, and so we hurry and fidget and excite ourselves, and do not consider that true devotion, accompanied by feelings of affection, is GOD'S gift, which must be awaited with confidence and humility, and not desired in order to gratify self-love. We want to be satisfied with our Communions; and we ought only to try to satisfy our LORD. In His satisfaction, we should find our own, after a nobler, more solid, more excellent manner than we can believe.

We wish to hear Mass and to communicate with saintlike fervour. The desire is good; but then we ought to begin by living like Saints; for it is folly to aspire to their tender and intense devotion, without imitating them in humility and mortification; and it is the grossest illusion to suppose that books will make up for the want of feelings. Love lies not in books, but in hearts.

After receiving the Blessed Sacrament, we should bring away more love than we took with us, and should therefore intend and resolve to be more recollected, more closely knit to GOD, more faithful to grace, more watchful over self, more loving, gentle, and patient, more careful in the fulfilment of duty, more generous towards GOD, more strong to bear the crosses of the day. This is love put in practice. And by communicating thus, and drawing these results from their Communions, the Saints attained the perfection of love.

I allow that this method is only fit for souls which have made some progress. But there are pure young hearts, ay, and hearty penitents, whom GOD Himself soon calls to it, attracting them to interior silence, and kindling them with sweet peaceful love at the time of Communion. Such souls need fear nothing: but at such times they should leave, not only books, but their own acts, and yield to the working of GOD.

It is true that sensible sweetness at Communion has its own time—should neither be sought nor clung to; nor, when no longer imparted, should it be pined and grieved for. There is much spiritual sensuality in such conduct; it is the love of CHRIST, not for His own sake, but for that of His consolations. When the privation does not result from our own fault, the Communion is none the worse, though it be devoid of comfort. Its peace is imparted, whether it be felt or no: and the heart is filled, however empty it may feel. Our state at Communion generally corresponds to our state in prayer; and the further we advance in mortification of self, the more we are weaned from all sweetnesses. If the heavenly food is then less delicious, it is more strengthening. The soul, in its trials, needs consolation less than strength, which latter is abundantly bestowed in those

Communions in which nothing seems to be imparted.

A Communion is not to be judged by present, but by subsequent effects. GOD soon leads some powerful, generous souls beyond sweetnesses, that He may give them what is more substantial. A Communion is excellent when it results in the thorough determination to correct our faults, deny ourselves, bear the inward and outward crosses sent by GOD, and give Him, according to our present state, due proofs of love and faithfulness. Such Communions as do not produce this effect are at least fruitless. Natural sensibility, imagination (and sometimes Satan) may have the chief share in the pleasure then enjoyed, which only serves to lull the vain and timid soul in dangerous illusion.

As to frequent Communion, the confessor must regulate that, with holy discretion. It must be a gradual work, advancing in proportion to the progress of the soul. As soon as a Christian sets himself diligently to work out his own salvation, he should be exhorted to communicate every month, without waiting till he is quite rid of his former habits: or, rather, in order to get rid of them more easily; and there may be reasons, such as occasions of strong temptations, or difficult duties, which render more frequent Communions desirable.

Weekly, and more than weekly Communion ought, regularly speaking, to be granted to those souls only, which are not attached to any venial sins, but are resolved to commit no intentional fault, and to obey the will of God in all things; and who moreover devote themselves to inward mortification and mental prayer, so far as their condition allows.

Daily Communion may be allowed to the same persons when it is evident that they are acquiring strength in the practice of virtue, and of fighting bravely with themselves; and are avoiding all that might in the slightest degree draw them away from recollectedness and union with GOD. As the spiritual life has its ordinary rate of progress, and as an enlightened director can easily perceive whether such souls are advancing or falling back, he ought to diminish the number of their Communions, if he perceives any laxity, which continues after they have received repeated warnings from him on the subject.

SEVENTH MAXIM.

Let intention be pure, and devotion simple and upright.

"*If thine eye be single, thy whole body shall be full of light.*"

VII.

OF PURITY OF INTENTION, SIMPLICITY, AND UPRIGHTNESS.

ALL the Fathers explain these words to refer to purity of intention, and understand them to signify, that if our object be pure, our actions will be righteous. As the eye guides, and in some sense enlightens the body, so the intention enlightens the soul; it guides its actions, and gives them their value for good or evil. Therefore as holiness of action depends on purity of intention, it is of serious importance that this subject should be understood: yet nothing is more difficult.

Intention lies in the deepest part of the human heart, so that, if we would unveil it as fully as is possible, we must be practised in the science of pondering on our own souls, examining their hidden motives, and penetrating their deep recesses. This is done by few persons, and in supernatural matters it can be duly performed only by the help of divine light, which must needs be sought always by diligent prayer.

Our self-love endeavours studiously to hide our intentions from ourselves. It does so with a view to its own interests; and succeeds only too well. We deceive ourselves in things innumerable, and we do it, though wilfully, yet so subtlely, that we scarcely perceive it. Few men are thoroughly honest with themselves; self ought to be the first object of mistrust, and therefore we ought to be on our guard against the devices of self-love, which are more abundant in matters of piety than in any thing else.

If, in order to know ourselves thoroughly, we must ascertain the true motives of our actions, and if, though they be deeply corrupt, we are so disposed to ignore this, and dissemble with ourselves, how few men are there who possess true knowledge of self?

The fact is, that we are thoroughly known by GOD alone, and that in the most essential point; namely, as to whether we are worthy of love or hatred in His eyes. We cannot be absolutely certain that any one of our actions is pleasing in His sight. This ignorance will remain with us through life, and therefore it will always be impossible for us to pronounce with perfect certainty concerning the purity of our intentions; for, if we were sure that they were pure, we should also know that our actions are holy, and consequently that we are in a state of grace. Therefore we must always say with David, "Cleanse Thou me from my secret faults;" therefore we have need to cry: "Who can tell how oft he offendeth?" This truth is in itself very grievous, and particularly painful to self-love, which is always seeking for assurance; but, according to the designs of GOD, it ought to humble us, and not to cast us into despair. If we cannot reach absolute certainty on this point, yet by study of self, and by humbly appealing to GOD, we may obtain a moral certainty sufficient to give us peace. But then we are to neglect no means for obtaining it.

What is purity of intention? GOD alone is its object; it is mingled with no self-interest. Intention may be not pure, and yet not thoroughly bad; it often happens that the chief intention is good, but is defiled by an accessory intention added to it. Thus a priest in his apostolic work chiefly intends the glory of GOD, but takes pleasure in the applause of men. Therefore, in the sight of GOD, the first intention and the action consequent on it are not perfectly holy and irreproachable.

We may judge by this example of the imperceptible sin which steals into almost all our works. If we were fully persuaded of that, how impossible would self-complacency become! And this is what GOD intends; for He saves us by humility, and not by confidence in our own merit.

What must we do to acquire this precious purity of intention? We must continually watch our motives, in order to cast aside not only the palpably bad, but the imperfect. But we only discern our imperfections as we advance, and as our spiritual lights increase. GOD increases our lights progressively, according to the use we make of them; He adapts them to our present needs, and to the degree of purity which He requires of us at the moment. By this means we gradually discover in our intentions those imperfections which at first we did not see, and which GOD Himself hid from us. For what beginner, with how good a will soever, could bear the sight of those actions which he believes to be his best, if GOD showed them to him such as they are in His own sight? it would be enough to cast him into the lowest depths of despondency.

To make myself better understood, I will give an example of this imperfect power of vision. The entrance to a spiritual life is often strewn by GOD with flowers; He fills it with sweetness and consolation, in order to detach the soul from all that is not Himself, and to facilitate the exercises of an interior life, which otherwise would prove repulsive. The soul, which never before knew anything so delightful, clings impetuously to these new pleasures. In order to enjoy them it gives up all else, yields itself to prayer and mortification, is only happy when alone with GOD, and cannot bear any interruption of communion with Him. If GOD absents Himself for a time, the soul is wretched, and cries to Him to return; seeks Him uneasily, and takes no rest till He be found.

Much imperfection unquestionably exists here. The motive is good: GOD is the object sought; but the intention is not pure, because spiritual sweetness and sensible enjoyment are sought besides. The soul does not now see this imperfection: GOD Himself hides it, and it would be imprudent in a spiritual director to reveal it. But when the soul has for some time been fed on this milk, and begins to grow strong, the times of GOD's absence will grow longer, and will become habitual. Then a light will be given to show the previous impurity of intention, and the soul will gradually learn to serve GOD for Himself, and not for His gifts. This light would have done harm at first, but will be useful then. And at every new step fresh light is received, which reveals the imperfections of the preceding state.

Therefore, instead of overwearying ourselves by scanning our intentions, we need only make good use of the light given by God. But, on the other hand, we must faithfully consult and follow that; and must immediately reject every imperfection which it makes known to us. Hereby we gradually attain to a purity of intention which is more or less perfect, according to God's will concerning us. For purity of intention is the measure of holiness, and is proportionate to the degree of light communicated by God, and to the faithfulness of our correspondence to the same. God indeed considers, not our actions in themselves, but our motives. Therefore the slightest action of the Blessed Virgin was of greater value in the eyes of God than the noblest works of other Saints, because her intention was incomparably pure.

Simplicity is identical with purity of intention. Therefore our Lord says: "If thine eye be single;" that is, if thy sight be directed to one only object, which is God. So that I might be silent concerning simplicity, and content myself with what has now been said concerning purity of intention. But it is desirable to show that simplicity, which few persons rightly understand, is the root and essence of all perfection. To this intent we must raise our minds to God Himself, and in the first place consider simplicity as it shows itself in Him.

That only which is infinite is perfectly simple; that only which is perfectly simple is infinite. All things finite are manifold or complex; and all things complex are finite. This rule has no exception. Therefore, perfect simplicity befits God only; and accounts for the infinity of His perfections. The being of God is infinite; because it is simple and all in all, without extension or division. His eternity is infinite: because it is simple, having neither beginning, middle, nor end, and excluding the very idea of duration expressed by a succession of instants; His power is infinite: because it is simple, extending to all things possible, and exercised without effort, by a pure act of will. His knowledge is infinite: because it is simple, and consists in one idea, which is the idea of God Himself, in which He always sees all that has been, is, and will be, and all that is to abide in the order of possibilities. The very essence of God is infinite, because it is simple; in Him essence is existence, attributes are one with themselves and with essence, and are distinguished only by definitions conceived according to our own weak imaginations.

So also with moral attributes. Though finite in their effects with respect to us, they are infinite in themselves, by reason of their simplicity; as, holiness, wisdom, goodness, justice, mercy. The end of all God's works is likewise infinite, because simple: it is to His glory that all things must concur. Minds exercised in reflection may follow out the sublime theory which I merely indicate.

As simplicity is the chief characteristic of the perfections, and designs, and works of God, we cannot wonder that it is the chief constituent of perfection in reasonable creatures. Being finite, they are incapable of physical simplicity, but not of moral simplicity; and this they are bound to make their one object.

With regard to the creature, simplicity is reduced to one point: namely, that GOD alone is to be the rule of idea and judgment, the aim of desire, the end of action and suffering; all is to refer to Him, His good pleasure is to be preferred to all things, His holy will alone is always to be sought, seen, and followed out. Much is contained in this short summary.

The soul is truly simple, when it has attained this single view of GOD, and is perfected in unity. Ineffable unity, which in some sort deifies us by a most entire moral union with Him Who is supremely and absolutely One. "*One to One,*" was the continual expression of a great contemplative. How deep a meaning lies in those few words! They express all the truth and perfection of holiness, and all the happiness of which it is the well-spring. God is One by a unity which befits Him, and Him alone. He is One, and necessarily draws all things into His own unity. He is One, and sanctifies all things by participation in His unity; He is One, and all creatures capable of being happy are only so by possession of His unity. Therefore, in order to be holy or happy, the soul must be one by adhesion of mind and heart to Him only, for Him only, without any turning back towards self. If, besides looking to GOD, it gazes upon self, in any way soever distinguishing it from GOD, with a sense of ownership that separates its interests from those of GOD, that soul is no longer one or simple in mind, but double, having two objects; and as long as it is in this state, it cannot possibly be immediately united to GOD: it is not so united in this world by faith; nor will it be hereafter, till purification has burnt away all its multiplicity.

Therefore, if we desire holiness and happiness,

let us aspire to simplicity and unity: study to simplify our views, by accustoming ourselves to look upon GOD alone: forget ourselves, to think of Him: have no will or interest but His: seek His glory alone: and find our happiness in His. This is the state of the blessed. We shall not be admitted to the sight and fruition of GOD, till we attain to this mind; let us do so on earth, as far as possible.

But how can we acquire this sublime simplicity, the very idea of which transcends all our conceptions? Let us pray the Most Holy Himself to undertake the work of our simplification; let us devote ourselves to Him with this intention. Our own exertions will never rid us of multiplicity. But the more GOD acts alone in us, and the more we yield to the operations of grace, the more we shall increase in simplicity, without seeing, or wishing to see our own progress.

Simplicity in understanding, from which GOD will banish much prejudice, many uncertain opinions, and doubts, and false judgments, substituting in their place most simple truth, from which, again, He will put aside suspicion, mistrust, and forecastings, the results of false prudence: and will gradually reduce our multifold cogitations to a gaze of simple intelligence.

Simplicity in the will, which will own but one desire, one fear, one love, one hatred, and one object of affection, tending towards that object with invariable rectitude and unconquerable strength.

Simplicity in virtues, which will all meet and mingle in charity, as far as the state of this present life allows. Simplicity in prayer, which will be, so to speak, one only act containing all acts in itself. And lastly, simplicity in conduct, which will be even, uniform, straightforward, and true, arising from one principle, and reaching onward towards one aim.

Uprightness is but another name for purity of intention and simplicity.

As Scripture tells us, "GOD made man upright;" turned towards Himself alone, with an inward yearning for nearness to, and union with Him. But man had the power of turning towards himself, was tempted, and fell. Thence arose original sin and its consequences, which gave prodigious impetus to this tendency towards self: to which, without GOD'S recalling grace, we cannot but yield.

I am aware that as long as a man retains sanctifying grace, he does not lose that essential uprightness which is necessary and sufficient for salvation. But every act of self-love, of self-complacency, of seeking one's own interest unsubordinated to the interest of GOD, is a deflection from that uprightness, which, however slight, may entail most grievous consequences. The danger of the least error of this kind is twofold: first, we can never, by our own strength, regain our former uprightness, however slightly we may have diverged from it; secondly, we have no power of stopping, nor of carrying our deflection to a given point, and no further. These two considerations ought to weigh with us so deeply as to prevent our ever taking one deliberate step out of the right way.

Let us thoroughly examine the character of our devotion, and ascertain whether it is pure, simple, and upright. And as it is possible that we may be blinded on the subject, let us pray, and ask advice, and profit by the light we receive from GOD. If we make good use of this, we shall receive it more abundantly, and insensibly acquire the purity of intention, simplicity, and rectitude, which are now, and always have been, so rare among persons professing piety.

EIGHTH MAXIM.

Follow the enlightening Spirit of Christ. Mistrust the blindness and treachery of the natural mind.

"*Trust in the Lord with all thine heart, and lean not unto thine own understanding.*"

VIII.

OF THE NATURAL SPIRIT AND THE SPIRIT OF CHRIST.

MOST devout persons are religious after their own fashion and according to their own ideas and caprices. Very small is the number of those who deny themselves thoroughly, and seek to follow no light but that of grace. Such a line of conduct, on which depends almost all progress in the interior life, is much more difficult to men than to women, because they trust more to their own judgment. If it be suggested to a man full of confidence in his own reason and good sense, that he should give up his natural spirit in order to enter into the ways of GOD, he does not understand or see the necessity of the thing proposed; he has no notion that the thoughts of GOD are higher than our thoughts, and His ways other than our ways. He supposes that he has the right to guide himself, and the power to guide others.

What is the consequence? We are never thoroughly subjected to the Spirit of GOD; we contradict it, and fight against it in ourselves and in the souls under our charge; we form false judgments concerning spiritual things and persons; we obstinately reject what is good, and approve what is evil, or else vary perpetually, so that there is nothing fixed and continuous in our principles or our direction.

But what is the natural spirit? It is human reason, in so far as it professes to judge of the things of GOD by its own light without recourse to the light of grace; it is natural sense which believes itself sufficient to set down maxims and rules of conduct in these matters, both for itself and others; and which forms plans and methods without either consulting GOD, or those who are set over us in His place. In order fully to understand this, we must lay down as a first principle, that supernatural light alone gives us knowledge of spiritual things, and of all that pertains to the operations of grace; that our ideas on these points are only correct so far as GOD Himself impresses them upon our souls; that by this means alone we rightly understand what is written concerning them in Holy Scripture, and in books treating on such matters; that without this light we cannot possibly distinguish, in ourselves or in others, between that which emanates from GOD, or that which springs from other sources.

Hence it follows, that if the spirit of man is to form right judgment on religious matters, it must be constantly dependent on the spirit of GOD, and fully persuaded of its own insufficiency and incapacity; it must have incessant recourse to prayer, or rather must exist in a state of habitual prayer.

It also follows that a true acquaintance with the secrets of the interior life is not to be acquired only by reading books on the subject, however correct and profound they may be; nor yet by the mere meditation in which a man simply calls his own reflections to his assistance; but light from on high must be drawn down by humble prayer. Otherwise he will not understand what he reads; or, presuming that he does so, will misunderstand. In general he who does not lead an interior life comprehends little of spiritual matters, and is unable to make proper use of the little that he does grasp. And moreover, even he who has an interior spirit, can only understand, in books, such things as he has himself experienced. All that is beyond his own state is unintelligible to him, unless light be given him whereby to comprehend it. And God, leading us by the dark paths of faith, will not give us that light for ourselves; but grants it to those whom He entrusts with the direction of others.

This knowledge, being infused, is only to be retained by humility, faithful correspondence to grace, and continual care to advance in piety. It is lost, if pride appropriates it to self, if prayer and other sustaining exercises are neglected, if too much scope is allowed to reasoning and curiosity, and if no curb is placed on the activity of the mind, which should be passive when it is to receive what God has to give. Nothing is more delicate than the spirit of God: it is infinitely pure, and refuses all intermixture of the natural spirit. Nothing is more difficult than to receive and preserve it in perfect purity, because we are so much inclined to mingle something of our own with it. Nothing requires more attention, watchfulness, and mistrust of self. Self-love and Satan make it their one business to injure and quench this spirit in our hearts, turning us aside from its pursuit, and depriving us of it by secret and imperceptible devices.

A volume would be necessary for the full delineation of the natural spirit, for the definition of its distinctive characteristics, and the history of its fatal effects. It is the oldest disease of the soul; it preceded original sin itself, and caused it in our first parents. They would not have sinned, had they not discussed the commandment of GOD, sought out the motives of His prohibition, and listened to the tempter's suggestions on the subject. The natural spirit taught them to scrutinise, and led them to disobey; to it they owed the loss of their original rectitude, and of their simplicity, and happy innocence; and the fatal acquaintance with evil previously unknown.

This disease is most universal, most deeply seated, most inveterate, most difficult to cure. It is a subtle poison, corrupting the whole substance of the soul, and infecting its good qualities and virtues. It is the enemy of GOD and of His grace, forbids entrance to His gifts, or robs us of them; all sins committed by man are either its effects or its punishment. Ordinary grace is insufficient for the cure of this disease. It resists the most violent remedies; and requires that they be of a special kind. Its cure demands long acute trials; and while life lasts, we cannot be certain that it is eradicated; one glance at self may revive the malady in the noblest of souls, and death alone frees them from it completely.

Self-will is another misery, which opened hell, as S. Bernard says. It follows closely after the natural spirit, and is, so to speak, its daughter; for our judgments precede and fix our affections. If the heart clings to objects from which the mind bids it turn, or feels aversion for what the mind would incline it to love, it is only when the mind is guided by pure reason or by grace, and both these lights come from GOD. So the fact remains that, not only deliberate sins, but sins of frailty, are all children of the natural spirit. Hence we may perceive how dangerous it is, and how much we ought to be on our guard against it.

The marks by which it is to be distinguished would easily be recognized, if seen by other eyes than one's own. We readily perceive them in others, and are but too clear-sighted about them. But the signs which strike us in others, escape our sight when we look at ourselves.

This spirit is confident, presumptuous, argumentative, ready and bold in judging; holds its own, and is unwilling to give way, because it is fully imbued with a sense of its own correctness. It always insists on seeing, and is loth to bend under the yoke of authority which compels it to believe. It is curious and must know everything; it does not perceive its own bounds, and, supposing all things to be within its depth, ventures to fathom all. It would not dare to assert its own infallibility; but it decides as positively as if it did so. Confession of error is its greatest humiliation; the more you endeavour to prove it in the wrong, the more it resists conviction; even when convinced, it refuses to yield, and it usually, through obstinacy, shuts its eyes to recognized truth.

Moreover, its sight is imperfect, and does not accept things as they are, but views them in the light most flattering to itself. It is deceitful, false, perverse, haughty, satirical, and contemptuous, continually on the watch against humiliation, loving adulation, and always secretly adding to the praises bestowed upon itself. And it is mistrustful, suspicious, ready to believe evil, to doubt good, and to give a bad interpretation to the most innocent things; always self-satisfied, never pleased with others, unless praised by them; always holding them to be in the wrong, as soon as they begin to contradict or blame.

Such, and still more horrible, are the features of the natural spirit. It would be shocked, could it see itself as it is; but the crowning point of its misery lies in that it is blind; and its wilful blindness increases by reason of its deformity. If you endeavour to open its eyes, you irritate and excite it; it rebels against you, and all you say in order to undeceive it, merely confirms it in its self-complacency.

The reason is, that, blind as it is, it fancies itself clear-sighted. The more it is mistaken with regard to itself, the more certain it feels that it does itself a justice which is refused it by others. Its blindness arises from the fact that it sees itself only by the false glare of pride, vanity, and presumption, which not only hides its vices and defects, but gives them the appearance of virtues. If it could consult reason, and, yet rather, grace, it would know itself rightly by means of the double lights; but it never does so, and inasmuch as it is a natural spirit, it is incapable of so doing.

In these words I depict almost all men, even those who profess piety and devotion, and a great number of those who think themselves interior and spiritual. The natural spirit, as regards religion, is the very same thing as the spirit of the Pharisees, of which our LORD drew so striking a picture. He attacked it strenuously by word, condemned it openly by act, and vouchsafed to be its victim, in order the more thoroughly to deter His disciples from it.

And yet unfortunately this spirit is very common among Christians, both lay and clerical. Those priests are possessed by it who look out for temporal advantage and the good opinion of men; who receive the great and rich with open arms and flattering words, while they deal harshly with the mean and poor; who exercise despotic rule over men's consciences; who parade great rigour and inflexible severity, exaggerating and condemning, and discovering sin in everything. This spirit also actuates those who are slaves to external practices, knowing the letter only, and not the spirit of the law; who have one set routine of prayers, and will on no account step beyond the circle they have drawn round themselves; who think nothing right but what they do, and are continually looking at their neighbours in order to blame them concerning every point in which they are unlike themselves; who, acquainted only with set meditation, which they perform in a dry manner, in which the heart has little share, condemn simple, humble prayer, and call it a barren and dangerous idleness; who boast themselves of a strained, affected kind of spirituality, the seat of which is not in the heart, but in the proud mind and deluded imagination.

In the devotion of all these people, the natural spirit is substituted for the spirit of God, or at any rate so mingled with it as to hinder their progress, bring discredit on piety, and scandalize worthy persons, who are thus disgusted with religion, as if it were responsible for an admixture which indeed it absolutely condemns.

The first thing to be resolved by any one who intends to lead a thoroughly Christian life, and to discard from his devotions all the faults just mentioned, is, not only to mistrust his natural spirit, but to study how to rid himself of it: fighting with it, and hunting it down without mercy. This war forms the chief part of that self-denial which our LORD enjoins on all who seek to follow Him.

But the natural spirit cannot fight against itself because it does not know itself. Reason, unless enlightened by faith and aided by grace, is but a feeble weapon. There is no known example of any philosopher who by his own reflections ever succeeded in ridding himself of his natural spirit. The slight conquests won in that way, far from weakening it, supply it with fresh strength, by reason of the vain complacency derived from victory.

It can by no means be overcome, except it be attacked with the arms of grace, and with prayer that GOD would aid the strife by His own Almighty hand. It must be laid before GOD as His mortal enemy, declaring that its utter destruction will be hailed as the greatest blessing. If this declaration is sincere and often reiterated, GOD will take the battle into His own hands, and teach us how to second Him. He will endue us with His own spirit, and we shall soon feel a sense of its presence. This spirit will gradually undermine and regulate the activity of our own. It will stop its discussions, quiet its agitations, rectify its ideas, correct its malignity, beat down its pride, cut away its propensity for grasping; and bring us by degrees to that state in which, like S. Paul, we may say: "I live; yet not I; but CHRIST liveth in me."

How is this done? That is one of the secret things of GOD; so perfectly inexplicable, that the human spirit cannot unravel it. All I can say is, that we soon perceive the first effects of the Divine work; we feel ourselves to be quite different persons. We know that the cause of the change is an interior spirit, communicated by GOD: but what is that interior spirit? How does it work? We know not.

The change at once produced by it in the ideas and affections is such, that it must have been felt to be understood. Scripture speaks of it as the birth of the new, inward, spiritual man, who, by his gradual development imperceptibly destroys the old man, and, when arrived at full vigour, slays him utterly. The nourishment of this new man is prayer: infused prayer, prayer never intermitted while reason retains its sway, and resumed on waking after the night's rest; prayer made within us, yet in some sort without our own act, and which, when once habitual, is maintained with little difficulty.

This is the unobtrusive weapon ever acting upon the natural spirit. Its work is aided by temptations, trials, contradictions, and humiliations. GOD employs all means to quell so formidable an enemy; even the prejudices and wickedness of men, the malice of Satan, and the threatening arms of His own justice. So Job says: "The terrors of GOD do set themselves in array against me." The soul seconds GOD in this war by yielding itself to His crucifying operations, and superadding the practiees of interior mortification.

It will be readily allowed that the natural spirit is as I have described it, blind, deceitful, and treacherous; that we ought to follow after the Spirit of CHRIST, which prevents us from walking in darkness, and gives us the light of life: that it is the intention of all who honestly serve GOD to follow that spirit; but it will be asked why so few do really follow it.

I make answer, that the number of those who honestly serve GOD is not so large as is supposed; not on account of hypocrisy or an intentional deceiving of others, but by reason of the prevalence of self-deceit. If men were so honest, would they flatter themselves? Would they spare themselves? Would they withhold from GOD so many things which they know He asks of them? Would they turn such a deaf ear to grace, and complain of its importunity? Would they use so many little devices for the reconciling of their own interests with those of God? Are they unconscious that He bids Christians deny themselves thoroughly and constantly? Do they do so? Honesty does at least accuse itself of its own shortcomings, humbles itself and repents, makes strenuous efforts for amendment, and prays unceasingly with that intent. And I appeal to honesty; let it answer me, or rather answer GOD, and that sincerely, on all these points.

So, likewise, I say that the intention men entertain of following CHRIST is generally vague, superficial, and speculative, without determinate object, not springing from the depth of the will, and not maintained in practice. He who would follow the spirit of CHRIST must needs be acquainted with it; but in order to such acquaintance, it must be studied; and in order to such study, one must enter into the mind of JESUS, and search out the feelings and dispositions of His soul. And who are those that dwell in the mind of JESUS? Who, again, are those who put in practice what they know of His mind, and are determined to carry to the utmost point their conformity with the Divine model? Such Christians are rare.

Most persons have not even the slightest idea of the spirit of JESUS; others are afraid of knowing too much about it, because they know themselves bound to conform their lives to it; and others are willing imperfectly to imitate a few of its features, but will not go so far as to attempt an entire resemblance.

What really was the mind of CHRIST, the spirit which gives us light, and guides us in the way of salvation? It was a perfectly interior spirit, by which He was constantly united to GOD His FATHER, devoted to His glory and His good pleasure; a spirit lifted infinitely beyond all perishable pleasures, riches, and honours; leading Him to choose and embrace poverty and obscurity, labour and suffering, humiliation and opprobrium; detached from all natural affections and feelings; always and in all things dependent on grace, and so submissive to its workings as never to think, or will, or desire, or do anything apart from it; a spirit, over which the Divinity to which it was hypostatically united exercised perfect sway, boundless authority, and constant influence; a spirit which maintained Him in a state of perfect devotion to His FATHER'S interests, of unreserved sacrifice to the claims of Divine justice, of utter humility, and continual mortification.

This was the spirit of CHRIST, which we, as

Christians, are bound to make our own. In this respect especially He is set forth for our pattern, as Head of the elect. GOD willed to show us in Him what we ought to be, and in order to serve as an example to us, the Eternal Word vouchsafed to assume our nature. Disciples are bound to tread in their Master's footsteps.

Some persons excuse themselves by saying that JESUS was GOD; but He offers Himself for our imitation, not as GOD, but as man. We shall never attain the perfections of the Divine Original; we are well aware of that, and it would be impiously absurd to profess to do so. But every man ought to endeavour to respond to his own especial grace, as CHRIST responded to His. GOD asks no more, but neither does He ask less.

It may be suggested that, as JESUS was GOD, all things were easy to Him. Certainly He could not sin, nor could He resist grace; nor was there in Him any obstacle to any virtue soever. And withal, He certainly endured a state incomparably more painful than that of all Martyrs and all Saints put together; human nature was overwhelmed and crushed in Him, under the fearful weight of GOD's vengeance on sin; if He was GOD-man, He certainly felt, and suffered all that a GOD-man could feel, and suffer. GOD does nothing in vain; and in the great design of the Incarnation and the redemption of mankind, all was ruled by infinite wisdom, and measured by exact justice. That which He required of CHRIST was proportionate to the grace and strength He had received.

Yet, if the sight of so perfect a pattern terrifies our cowardice, let us turn our eyes on mere men: on S. Paul, for instance, who called on Christians to be followers of him, as he also was of CHRIST. Let us study the mind and feelings of the Apostle in his Epistles, and impress them on our own life. I shall be told that he was a man converted by extraordinary grace, a chosen vessel, concerning whom GOD had high designs, and on whom He lavished His bounties. I make answer that S. Paul was neither sanctified by his apostleship nor by his election, but by his correspondence to GOD'S calling. And in this only, in his good use of GOD'S grace, are you asked to imitate him. Who hinders you? Was not S. Paul a blasphemer and a persecutor, when GOD cast him down to the ground? When grace appeals to you, say, as he did: "Lord, what wilt Thou have me to do?" And then, do the bidding of grace as faithfully as he did.

Will you have patterns still more within your reach? Read the lives of Saints. There have been Saints of all ages, all ranks, all conditions. Many retained baptismal innocence; others had been great sinners; they were subject to the same passions, and habits, and temptations, as ourselves: and sometimes to greater; that is, they had as many or more obstacles to surmount, and it is remarkable that the Church never won more Saints than in those first ages when the profession of Christianity was a pledge of martyrdom.

Then you will complain that they were Saints. What other models would you have? Whereunto are you called, save to holiness, like theirs? They were sanctified only by living as true disciples of CHRIST, and following the spirit, and teaching, and example of their Master.

But whence do these vain objections arise? From the natural spirit; and nothing more clearly shows its blindness. In all arts the best models are sought out, studied with extreme care, and sedulously imitated. And shall we complain of the too great perfection of our models in the chief of all arts, that art which only is important, the art of rightly ruling one's life, becoming well-pleasing in GOD's sight, and worthy of His eternal fruition? What monstrous contradiction! We refuse to put on the spirit of CHRIST, because it would involve the putting off our own. As if an artist refused to assume the manner of a great master, rather than depart from his own worthless style. But so long as men will not give up their natural spirit, they must give up the idea of being real Christians, for there is no real practical Christianity, except that which consists in thinking and acting according to the spirit of CHRIST.

NINTH MAXIM.

Take no account of external things; seek strenuously after those blessings which are to be found within.

"*Commune with your own heart and in your own chamber, and be still.*"

IX.

OF THE OUTWARD AND INWARD MAN.

THE natural man, the old man, the man of sin, is called the outward man on account of his natural bias to objects of sense; and the spiritual man, the new man, that man according to grace, is called the inward man, because, dwelling apart in himself with GOD, he only cleaves to things invisible and supernatural.

Sensible objects hold a marvellous sway over man. Their power begins in childhood, when pleasures and pain arise from these sources only. It develops with age; the soul is keenly affected by all that strikes it from without; admiration and envy are excited by those accidents which raise some persons above their fellows, as, nobility, office, honour, and riches. Men look on these things as truly good, bestow their esteem and love upon them, seek only to enjoy them, and believe that happiness lies in the possession, and misery in the absence of these advantages.

The work of sense and of corrupt nature is already far advanced, when grace comes forward to destroy it, and raise a very different building on its ruins. She teaches us that we are true Christians only in so far as we despise sensible things, and apply ourselves to things spiritual; ceasing to be outward men, and becoming altogether interior men; so that the Christian who is interior in certain respects, at intervals, and as it were, by fits and starts, is imperfect, while the perfect Christian is interior in all things and at all times; and aiming at an interior life and at Christian perfection are one and the same thing.

This is a hard lesson for nature to learn. Some refuse to accept it at all; others listen with much ado, resist for a length of time, put it in practice as little as possible, and that with great repugnance. It is received and fully and faithfully observed by very few persons, and even these pass through long and painful struggles in the first place. The wisdom from above is so different from the wisdom of the flesh; it is so difficult to rise to the noble philosophy of grace.

The Christian is, in this respect, a supernatural being, intended, not only for immortality, but for the eternal fruition of GOD; and that fruition passes all his thoughts, desires, and hopes, and even the exigencies of his nature: it is His Creator's pure gift; promised by revelation, and known to him by faith alone. He is prepared for this end by other blessings of the same order, which are called graces. The chiefest of these is habitual, and is called sanctifying grace; the others are actual graces, which tend either to the recovery of sanctifying grace, if it be lost, or to its preservation and increase. The object of these graces is to give a supernatural character both to the state of the Christian and to the free acts by which he may and must merit the fruition of GOD.

The Christian is born into this world, and dwells therein for a certain time. But he is not of the world, it is not his, he is a stranger and a sojourner. Present and sensible advantages are not his object; as S. Augustine says, he may use them, but not enjoy them; that is, GOD grants them to him for the necessities of his animal life, but his heart is not to cling to them, nor to rest on them as its final end. The true riches of the Christian on earth are, grace, close communion with GOD, and everything which fosters supernatural life within him: and those things only are real evils which weaken that life, or deprive him of it.

External good and evil, therefore, are to him properly speaking, neither really good, nor really evil; but things called good may become evil, and the reverse, according to the use he makes of them. It is not so with interior good and evil. These are essentially connected with his supernatural state; that is, with his state as a Christian, and his eternal happiness or misery.

Consequently, he ought to be indifferent to sensible good and evil, because in themselves they are indifferent things, which are profitable or hurtful to him, according to his interior dispositions. And, on the other hand, the whole strength of his mind and will must be devoted to the acquirement and eschewal of such good and evil things as are of a supernatural order, and which can never be indifferent to him, on account of their intimate connection with his last end.

All Christians are much of one mind touching this great truth, as far as theory is concerned;

but almost all follow other principles in practice. I am not alluding to those who thirst passionately for riches and honours and pleasures, and consider all means as lawful, whereby their desires may be obtained. These are Christians only in name, and as long as they continue in such a mind, they they have no pretensions to being so in deed.

Bnt, among the remainder, are there many who are not proud of noble birth and title? Or who, having it in their power to aspire to honours and dignities, do not wish to obtain them, use many exertions for the purpose, feel delighted when their plans succeed, and unhappy when they are frustrated? Or who do not envy successful rivals? Or who, satisfied with an insignificant position, make no attempt to rise, wait quietly till others think of them, and are not annoyed at being forgotten? Or who, in order to rise in life, make use of none but strictly honourable means? Or who look on offices and employments solely as concerning the common weal, and not chiefly as regards private advantage?

Touching riches, I pass over the countless number of men in all ranks of life who obtain them by means forbidden by uprightness and true religion, and concerning which so much self-deceit prevails. But I ask: Are Christians often to be found, who, having wherewith to support their families decently and sufficiently, wish for nothing further? Are they apt to believe that they do possess a sufficiency, or are they not always fancying that they have not enough? And is it not true that pride accompanies opulence, and that self-esteem increases in proportion to riches?

As to pleasures, even of those permissible (for I speak not of others), how much sensuality is to be found amongst Christians, how much care, how much daintiness! How eagerly these pleasures are sought out! How passionately they are enjoyed! How artfully they are invented, and varied, and multiplied! How careful men are to have all their comforts about them, to avoid the slightest disagreeables, to flatter their flesh, and bestow on it all the gratification for which it is so ravenous?

People think themselves good Christians, if, in all these matters, they keep within the letter of the law, and run into no excess. But this is very different from the mind of a perfect Christian.

He stifles every germ of ambition in his heart; he not only does not desire honours, but fears, abhors, and avoids them: remembering the words of the Gospel: "That which is highly esteemed among men is abomination in the sight of God." Positions of dignity appear to him to involve a great burden for the conscience, great duties to be fulfilled, and great account to be rendered. If birth or Providence call him to fill such posts, he appears in the simple garb of modesty and humility; he is watchful against himself and against the snares laid for him on all sides; he continually examines his conduct with most scrupulous attention, thinking himself answerable for all the good he does not do, and all the evil he does not hinder. If he is of low estate, he thanks God for it, and rejoices in it, as being a state more conformable to the Gospel, happier, more innocent, more conducive to salvation; and he is far from making any attempts to change it. He not only hates honours, but wishes for humiliations, because he knows and feels their value; and if they befal him, he receives them as favours from heaven, and thinks himself happy if despised, cast out, slandered, and persecuted, like his Master.

As to riches, the true Christian, taught by the Gospel, regards them as thorns and encumbrances which turn him away, in spite of himself, from more important matters; he possesses them without cleaving to them, uses them with extreme moderation, divides them with the poor, whose steward he feels himself to be, and diminishes his own expenses as much as possible in their favour, believing that his superfluities are necessary to them, and that all he can spare belongs to them. If he is poor, he is glad of his poverty, pleased to feel its effects, and to want sometimes for necessary things; he would not allow in himself the least desire of greater competency. He feels it too great a privilege thus to bear some resemblance to his LORD, Who chose a state of poverty wherein to be born, to live, and to die.

The holy severity of the Gospel is his rule in the use of pleasures. He seeks out none for their own sakes, and passes through natural and necessary gratifications as through fire. In no respect will he indulge the flesh; he mortifies it ingeniously, granting no quarter to predilections, and conquering repugnances; but all with holy liberty, unaffectedly and discreetly. No Saint, that is, no true Christian, ever treated his body indulgently; and it has been the general practice of such men to bring it into subjection by fastings, and watchings, and macerations, which terrify our self-indulgence and cowardice. They all considered it an essential duty to bear about in their body the dying of the LORD JESUS.

Such, with regard to this world's goods, have perfect Christians always been, even when living in the world; for I do not limit what I have now said to those who have embraced voluntary poverty and chastity, and who have altogether left the world for solitary places and monasteries.

Let not those be alarmed at this picture, who, as S. Bernard says, see but the cross we have to bear, and see not the unction which we receive withal; let them not fancy that a true Christian's life is one of perpetual constraint and torture. The licentious and the impious love to depict it under such hideous colours, in order to excuse themselves for having turned their backs upon it. But they blaspheme that which they know not; they intentionally deceive themselves, and desire to deceive others.

No; the true Christian, following out the moral teaching of religion, is not constrained and tortured; he does, indeed, do violence to his nature, but not to his mind or his heart. He is perfectly convinced that he ought to do what he does, and he delights to do it. Through grace, he despises, hates, and avoids the sweet and false advantages of which he deprives himself. GOD has raised his soul above such things: He has shown him the nature of true honours, riches, and pleasures; and that sight prevents him from beholding elsewhere anything but vanity and vexation of spirit. In the school, first of wisdom, and then of experience, the Christian learns that to serve GOD is to reign, that the possession of virtue constitutes wealth, and that true pleasure consists in peace of mind.

The Christian made this discovery when he turned his thoughts upon his own soul, and reflected on past errors, and acknowledged that he had never found happiness in the enjoyment of this world's goods: when he listened to GOD in the silence of meditation and prayer. It was then that he really saw the nothingness of earthly things, and understood that they were capable indeed of exciting his passions, but never of satisfying his heart. Then a deep secret touch of grace taught him that man's true happiness lies in GOD; and that, in order to enjoy and possess it, he must give up, or at least give up his love for, all other joy. From that time forth, all things have seemed insipid, except prayer and communion with GOD; the world has been crucified to him and he to the world; he has been attracted to GOD alone; he has sought Him, and found Him within his own soul, which is GOD'S very temple.

Who shall express the delight of finding within one's self what had vainly been sought elsewhere? Of discovering the real, infinite, inexhaustible treasure, the treasure which only is capable of filling the immense capacity of the heart, or, rather, for which the heart is too small, and wherein it plunges and loses itself. After feeling what this happiness is, how should he dream of leaving GOD for created things, and forsaking the fountain of living waters for broken cisterns, which can hold no water?

It is perfectly impossible; unless, with monstrous faithlessness, he gradually leaves the interior path on which he had entered. You may make meditation, and even do it well, and yet keep up some connection with the senses and with matters which please them; but you cannot make true contemplative prayer for any length of time, without breaking off intercourse with created things. For the property of such prayer is, to concentrate all the affections on God, and to allow us to love nothing save through Him, in Him, and for Him.

Make the attempt, Christian soul, and you will see if I speak truly. If you tell me that it is not in your power to enter on this path of prayer, I answer, on God's behalf, that He is ready to second your good will, and to bring you into it, if you prepare for it by such means as depend upon yourself. Have such a good will; and, as you cannot assure yourself of having it, ask it of God: and that instantly. This very request would be the beginning of it; and how should God refuse you what He inspires you to ask? If few persons possess it, it is because few desire it, and those who do ask it, for the most part, fear to obtain it. God reads the heart; He sees whether we respond to the feelings which He breathes into it, and always hearkens to those who do so respond. But He hearkens to those only. Others reproach Him, as if He rejected their prayers: I pray in vain, they say, I ask in vain for a good will; God does not give it me. He will one day show them that, if they had it not, they themselves only were to blame. I repeat, that a soul which co-operates to the best of its power with present grace, must infallibly obtain greater graces from moment to moment; and if it carries on this co-operation steadily, it will certainly attain to all the holiness which God expects of it.

TENTH MAXIM.

Listen to Him who teacheth thy heart without sound of words. Receive His peace, and guard it faithfully.

"I will speak to his heart."

X.

OF RECOLLECTION, ACTIVE AND PASSIVE.

THE delights of GOD are with man; He loves to speak to his heart; and therefore the secret of a spiritual life consists in knowing how to retire into one's own heart and dwell therein with GOD. How does GOD convert sinners? By calling them to enter into their own hearts: as soon as they do so, their sins appear before their eyes, and cause them great remorse; healthful thoughts arise in their minds; good feelings crowd into their souls. If they do not shrink from dwelling within themselves: if they do not flee from themselves, and seek relief or diversion in outward objects, a change will soon take place in their lives.

If a soul is well meaning, but unsettled, giddy, prone to many faults, clinging to certain venial sins: or if, having once been fervent, it has fallen into laxity, GOD makes use of these same means to bring it out of imperfection, or restore it from lukewarmness. He calls it into itself. There it hears reproaches, and the reproaches are just, gentle, and severe. If it listens with a docile spirit, it improves, and if it continues thus dwelling within itself with God, it will infallibly advance from strength to strength.

This turning to listen to the voice of grace within the heart is called recollection. The term expresses that act whereby the soul gathers and collects into itself those powers of attention which had been scattered and divided amongst divers objects. There are two sorts of recollection; one, active: which is the work of the will aided by grace; the other, passive: which is the gift of God. The latter is usually the reward of the former, after that has been faithfully practised for some space of time.

The first object of active recollection is the custody of the senses, especially sight and hearing; which are, as it were, the windows through which the soul looks out and busies itself with passing matters. Whilst exclusively attentive to external things, it cannot watch over itself, nor give heed to the internal teacher that seeks to instruct and correct it; it cannot so much as hear his words.

Therefore it is necessary early to accustom one's self to exercise great restraint over one's eyes, so as to acquire the power of turning them, not only from dangerous, but from distracting and amusing objects. By staying the restless mobility of the eyes, we obtain an efficacious means whereby to stop the flightiness and moderate the vivacity of our imagination; to prevent the arising of passion, and to set the soul in a condition which is very favourable to meditation, and still more so to prayer.

Eagerness to hear and know everything is not less fatal to solid piety; and it cannot be too carefully repressed. By means of the ears, the soul is taken up with a variety of things which afterwards distract, and fill it, in spite of itself, even at the time of prayer. Therefore we choose quiet places for meditation; therefore the tumult of cities naturally distracts the mind, while the silence of woods and fields invites to recollection. Besides, unprofitable curiosity leads to long, frequent, and uncharitable conversations, impertinent questions, suspicions, conjectures, hasty judgments, endless discussions on public and private affairs; in these things GOD is often offended, and they are incompatible with a spirit of prayer and true devotion.

So then he who would prepare himself for an interior life must give up the habit of constantly running after rarities of all sorts: pictures, statues, fine buildings, festivities, and public representations, which move the soul too violently, and in which many things concur to inspire false pleasures or dangerous passion. He ought not to be eager to know the gossip of a town, the family affairs of others, or public news; nor ought he to occupy his time in such matters, unless obliged to do so by position or personal interest. Not that one may not casually and occasionally see and hear such things without evil result, but they are not to be longed for, nor clung to, and their place in the mind must be kept subordinate to more important subjects.

Mental curiosity is no less to be feared; and he who would attain the habit of recollectedness, must learn to keep it within due bounds. By mental curiosity, I mean that immoderate desire of learning and knowing, which causes people to study various sciences eagerly, and generally superficially: to read every book as it comes out, rather for the sake of showing off than of improvement. Recollectedness cannot, I think, be compatible with such a disposition, which rather is the sign of a shallow mind.

Let us not fall into this defect; or, if we are prone to it, let us strive against it. We must be satisfied with such learning as is necessary or suitable to us individually; we must not read a book simply because it is new or much talked of; and even as to religious works, those we study should be few and good. We must not be like those persons who want to have every book of that kind, going continually from one to another, without finishing any. This is not the place to dwell on the manner of reading such works to advantage; I will only say that there is nothing with which curiosity ought to have less to do.

There is another temperament which, at first sight, seems favourable to recollectedness, and yet is very adverse to it. It is that of low-spirited persons. Their imagination clings closely to certain objects, frames numberless chimeras from the recollection of the past, and the expectation of the future; building a multitude of castles in the air, with all due circumstance of place, person, and situation. These romantic imaginations enable their possessors to live in a state of constant occupation; they can sit alone in their room, and converse with the whole world. Persons of this disposition like solitude; they are silent and musing; they keep their senses under control, or rather, make little use of them, for they take little heed of outward things. They seem to be recollected, but are only preoccupied; and such as these find the greatest difficulty in acquiring an habitual sense of God's presence.

The practice of ejaculatory prayer is an excellent means for the acquirement of recollectedness, because it tends to recal us often to ourselves and to God. It is a very good thing to bind one's self to the custom; but yet such prayers must not be made a matter of routine. They should rise from the heart rather than the lips, and are best when they consist of a simple turning of the soul towards God, unaccompanied by any words expressed or understood. We cannot take too much pains to acquire this method of prayer. If it becomes daily more frequent, and grows into a habit, it disposes the mind to that prayer which is without ceasing.

Whether we are reading, or meditating, or repeating vocal prayers, it is good to pause from time to time, and let the soul quite suspend its own action to give place to the working of God. If we feel at all touched by grace at such moments, we cannot do better than give way to it, and quietly enjoy the feelings God gives us; and when that impression has passed away, we can resume our book or our prayers.

These passing touches are a small beginning of infused prayer, to which we ought to correspond very faithfully; they are momentary visits, wherein God communicates Himself. And, short though they are, they do us more good than any of the thoughts and affections wherein the soul speaks to itself. Why do we read, or pray, except for the purpose of attaining to union with God? So, when He comes, and bestows on us a certain secret sense of His presence, we have what we desire. We should therefore yield to this sense as long as it lasts. It would be irreverent to go on with our previous occupation; by so doing, we should deprive ourselves of the effect of His visits, and should render them less frequent. S. Francis de Sales strongly recommends this practice to his daughters, and even bids them stop the recital of their office on such occasions.

Passive recollection is not a transitory visit from God, but an habitual sense of His presence in the soul. We feel that presence; we cannot entertain any doubt about it; and its effects are so deep and sweet, as to be plainly due to God alone. The soul is filled and strengthened by an indefinable calm and peace, and suspension of its natural powers, with which no natural pleasure of any kind is to be compared. These feelings are not bestowed on the soul at the time of prayer only, but accompany it in almost every act. Whatever may be our situation, our occupation, or our company, we feel, when we turn our thoughts within, that God is present in our souls as a faithful companion.

This is not to be treated as a dreaming fancy by those who never felt anything of the kind, and cannot imagine what it is: those who do so would contradict the doctrine of the Saints and the experience of all interior livers. Nor is it to be feared that this be an illusion of Satan: for that cannot take place respecting this habitual presence of God, with which imagination has nothing to do.

The principal effect of this recollectedness is to turn the soul inward, detaching it from external things, and deadening their effect. I do not mean that the soul thus ceases to feel; this recollectedness is not ecstasy, depriving it of ordinary sensation; but it does not pause or dwell on what it feels, because it is restrained inwardly by a charm more powerful than anything that would attract it from without. By this means God withdraws the soul from communion with creatures, and binds it wholly to Himself, so that it feels itself alone with God, and pays no attention to any other object. This recollectedness is, properly speaking, the entrance of the interior life, and is the surest sign that a soul is in the passive state.

It is at first such as may be felt; because the sense of it is necessary, in order to detach the soul from conversation with created things, and to inspire it with contempt for the pleasure derivable from them; but when this effect is produced, recollectedness leaves the surface of the soul, and sinks deeper. It is no longer felt; it is only noticed, because for a time we retain the habit of thinking about it; and at last we cease to perceive it, because, as we advance, we go out of self and enter into God, and are less taken up with what passes within ourselves.

As this habitual presence of God is the foundation of all the graces which He afterwards bestows on the soul, we cannot be too sedulous in preserving it. The love which the soul feels towards God in these early days, leads it to assiduity in prayer and other pious exercises, reception of the Sacraments, and practice of bodily mortification; but in addition to these things, it is necessary to withdraw altogether from created things, and have as little to do with them as possible. As far as may be, it is necessary to lay aside most of those good works which would draw the soul to external interests; for the one thing needful in this state, is an entire yielding of one's self to the operation of God;

and this requires retirement, silence, and cessation from business, except such as concerns the duties of one's position, which takes precedence of all other things. Such good works will subsequently be resumed, and even multiplied, when God gives the signal for them, and they no longer involve the risk of distracting the mind. Moreover, the senses are now to be allowed no liberty, no curiosity is to be indulged, all idle thoughts are to be cast out of the mind, the heart is to be kept free from all attachment: all things, indeed, are to be put aside which may break or suspend our intercourse with God.

Let it not be supposed that this is painful. As long as sensible recollectedness lasts, nothing is difficult: God asks of us what He wills, in a manner so sweet and persuasive, that it is as it were impossible to refuse; we receive so many graces from Him that we feel unable to do enough in return; in fact, we are in the first fervour of love, and eager to prove to God that we do love Him. So that a person in the state of passive recollectedness, finds those practices very easy, which are difficult to observe in active recollection, and which are apparently and really great sacrifices, on account of their continuity. Hours spent in prayer seem short as minutes: the pleasures of the world taste insipid; unavoidable conversations become fatiguing; companionship, formerly delightful, grows uncongenial. Such a person is inclined to refuse satisfaction to the absolute cravings of nature, and yields to them regretfully. What has caused this wonderful change? A faint foretaste of the happiness of heaven. If this is the beginning of the spiritual life, what will be its consummation?

One word more. You want to be taught concerning the things of GOD; therefore you consult men, and the writings of men; and you do not apply to Him Who in one moment gives light to the humble soul, teaching it without sound of words, and imparting more in one single contemplation than could be obtained in many years from the most spiritual of men. You weary and worry your mind in order to be recollected in prayer; and nothing is really necessary for the purpose except a good will, and the use of such measures as shall prepare the soul aright: for it is absurd to try to be recollected at the time of prayer, if the mind is distracted at other moments. You seek to make your prayer, by your own efforts; GOD makes it within the soul, so soon as, convinced of our powerlessness, we cease from action on our own part, and yield to His; He Himself calls us to this cessation, when He intends to act in us. You wish to enjoy peace, and you agitate and distress yourself to obtain it; you grieve at not feeling it, while you are doing all that is likely to drive it away; and you do not remember that the GOD of peace dwelleth neither in agitation nor turmoil, but causes Himself to be felt like the soft breath of zephyr, which is produced by, and which maintains a state of, calm.

You seek self while you assume that you seek GOD; therefore you find Him not.

O! how astonished some persons would be if they knew how little labour is required for the attainment of simple recollectedness! But man is jealous of his own powers of action, and loves to attribute all things to himself. GOD is infinitely more jealous of His, and will have all attributed to Him. This is the cause of all mistakes concerning the interior life, and of the poor success of our attempts. GOD does nothing in him who fancies himself to be something, and who seeks to owe all to his own labour; but He acts, well pleased, on a soul which dwells, quietly humble, in His presence, attracting Him by its desires, counting not on its own efforts, awaiting all from His loving kindness. In the moral as in the physical world, GOD brings all things out of nothing. We must humble ourselves, yea, empty ourselves, before Him; and He will cause us to feel the effect of His power.

ELEVENTH MAXIM.

Deal with thy God as a child with its Father.

"*Wilt thou not from henceforth cry, My Father, Thou art the guide of my youth?*"

XI.

OF A CHILDLIKE SPIRIT.

It should seem that nothing could be easier or more usual for Christians, than to look on God as their Father, and act simply and trustfully with regard to Him. It is the very spirit of the new covenant, and is that which distinguishes it from the old. A fundamental dogma of our religion is, that God the Father has adopted us in His Son Jesus Christ, and raised us to the supernatural position of His children. This position makes us heirs of God, joint heirs with Christ, and gives us a right to heaven as our country, and the eternal fruition of God as our inheritance. The appellation, child of God, presupposes and recals to our minds the chief points of the faith: is the foundation of hope, and the paramount motive of love.

Yet nothing is rarer among Christians than these filial feelings towards God: almost all are more inclined to fear than to love Him. They find it exceedingly difficult to practise thorough confidence in Him and unreserved yielding up of self. The thing least known, and least faithfully observed in the spiritual life, and most difficult to human nature, is the casting all our care upon Him, in firm faith that nothing can be ordered for us by Him, which shall not work our good, unless we ourselves prevent it.

This arises from self-love, which persuades us that our interests are safe only so long as we have them in our own hands. We cannot make up our minds to trust them to God, to look on Him as our Father, and to believe in His love. We think He deals with us as a father, only when He caresses us, sends us sweet things, and gives us all we please to ask. But when, to teach us to love and serve Him for His own sake, without self-interest, He withdraws the comforts of which we have made ill use, refuses what would injure, and offers us what is useful, but what we will not accept: then we cease to consider Him a father; we see in Him a harsh pitiless master; His service is repulsive; we are perpetually tempted to give it up; our spiritual guides find great difficulty in holding up our steps that they slip not; and we have much ado to obey them, when they take God's part against us.

And yet so it is, that God never shows Himself more truly a father, than in the trials He sends us; crosses are the most precious favours He can bestow on us in this world; the more He lays on those who have given themselves to Him, the more He shows His love towards them. Was not Christ His beloved Son, in Whom He was well pleased? How did He deal with Him throughout His human life? Was He less His Father, when He gave Him up into the hands of wicked men, when He seemed to forsake Him on the Cross, and suffered Him to die in torture and in shame? Surely not: and it may truly be said, that if Calvary was the scene of CHRIST'S love for His Father, it was also the place where the FATHER'S love for His Son was the most clearly proved. Judge by the consequences. Certainly all the glory, and power, and blessing which our LORD possesses, as man, He owes to His Cross. "Ought not CHRIST," saith He, "to have suffered these things, and to have entered into His glory?" His Father required that temporary proof of obedience at His hands, that in His turn He might give Him an eternal proof of His magnificence in rewarding it.

Consider the education of a child. While weak and tender, he is nursed, carried about from place to place, petted, indulged, and soothed. But when he grows bigger, he is placed under rule; he is obliged to do things which are unpleasant, and of which he does not as yet see the use; he is broken in to obedience, and habituated to conquer his desire, and follow the guidance of reason; when necessary, he is treated severely, threatened, and chastised. Why? but in order to draw out his powers, make a man of him, and prepare a useful and happy life for him in the future.

GOD acts in the same manner towards His children. He intends them for citizens of the heavenly Jerusalem. When they begin to give themselves up to Him, He makes the greatest allowances for their weakness. He lavishes sweetness and comfort upon them, in order to win their hearts; He makes all things easy to them; He puts temptation away; He pleases them, and, as it were, makes Himself a child with them. But when they grow stronger, and are capable of receiving solid lessons in the interior life, He adopts another plan: attacks nature, and pursues all its defects and vicious propensities, sparing none. He prescribes difficult duties, and requires their fulfilment with extreme severity. The language of grace is no longer tender and persuasive; it is strong, imperious, and threatening; the slightest resistance is rigorously punished. He fits His exercises, trials, and temptations to their strength and condition; and, the more He has endowed them with powers natural and supernatural, the more He demands of them, till they are moulded to all virtues, and have passed through all degrees of holiness. And when they have reached that point of perfection to which He desires to bring them, their spiritual education is finished; He removes them into His kingdom, where He crowns their struggles and obedience, and makes them everlastingly partakers of His glory.

Thus, then, the interior life, in its whole course, is an education paternal and divine, inspired and ruled by love. GOD, on His side, perfectly fulfils the part of a Father. Let us endeavour to do all we ought as children of such a Parent.

And let us take children for our patterns once more. What are the feelings which a well-disposed child entertains for his father? In the first place, great simplicity, ingenuousness, and candour. The child has no notion of concealment or dissimulation with his father: he opens his heart to him, and tells him all he feels. We ought to do the same with GOD. In fear, or joy, or sorrow, we should go to Him with the openness and simplicity of children. He knows better than we do what is passing within us; but He likes us to speak to Him about it: He desires to be our friend and confidant. We should not even fear sometimes to address Him with loving reproaches; such holy liberty is agreeable to Him; and nothing displeases Him more than cold reserve.

The next point in a child's disposition is confidence. Timid and distrustful with others, he places boundless reliance in his father. He knows that his father loves him, cares for him, labours for him, plans for him, only, and has no other aim in view but his happiness. Therefore he neither cares nor troubles himself about his own welfare, but simply trusts to his father, who provides for his wants, and his harmless pleasures, forestals his slightest wishes, and reads them in his eyes. He knows, not by reasoning, but by instinct and experience, that his father means everything for his good: advice, lessons, correction, restraint, severity, and even apparent injury.

O! how safe we should feel, if we had but equal confidence in our heavenly Father, Who deserves it infinitely more than any earthly parent! if we would leave to His providence the care of our spiritual interests: expecting to attain salvation and perfection from His grace much more than from our own efforts: fully convinced that He arranges and orders all things for our good: whether they be commands which curb our passions inconveniently, or duties painful of fulfilment, or sorrows and troubles sent by Him, or secret providences, whereby He disconcerts our plans, crosses our designs, and overthrows our undertakings. If we believed these things, how much God would be glorified by our confidence, and what peculiar and especial care and protection He would bestow upon us!

Obedience is the next point in a child's disposition: obedience, based on love, not on fear or self-interest; embracing all its father's will, and not considering whether the performance of it is easy or difficult, pleasant or disagreeable; generous, ready, bold obedience, free from excuses and complaints; satisfied with the pleasure of giving pleasure to a dear and respected father.

Do most Christians obey God on this wise? Far from it. Why not? Because they forget that God is their Father, and look on Him in quite another light. Some fear damnation more than they desire salvation; because they are more struck by the idea of hell-fire than by that of the joy of heaven. Fear is the root of their obedience; they look on God as a harsh master and a severe judge.

Now, fear has power to keep us from evil, but not to lead us to good; it is a curb, but not a spur. It is the beginning, but only the beginning, of wisdom. God does not intend us to dwell in it; from fear we ought to pass on to love. In fact, we are not fearing God when we only fear His chastisement; and we do not obey Him according to His will when we only yield to His warnings. So that this obedience is as imperfect as its motive. It allows the full weight of the yoke to be felt, and does not remove from the heart a secret desire of casting it off. It limits itself to the letter of the law; and, as men naturally interpret it in their own favour, its obligations are often imperfectly fulfilled.

Others do indeed consider God as their rewarder; they serve Him for hope's sake. But they care less for Him than for the good things He promises them. In looking forward to and hoping for the fruition of GOD, they consider their own happiness more than they love Him. They are actuated by self-interest, and think of little else.

This motive has its advantages, for it incites them to well-doing; but it is not sufficiently pure; and their obedience, having no other stay, is weak and tottering, and often painful. True faith, which works by love, has very little influence on their conduct; the good and evil things of this present time weigh in their minds against the sense of good things to come. Therefore they find great difficulty in the practice of virtue, which consists chiefly in the contempt of temporal prosperity and the endurance of adversity; and they are hardly proof against some refined temptations, the victory over which is reserved to the love of GOD.

Not in fear, nor self-interest, but in love, is rooted the true principle of that obedience which is due to GOD: and nothing is fitter to inspire us with such love, than the paternal character which GOD vouchsafes to assume.—From all eternity He has loved me, not merely as His creature, but as His child: He tells me in His Scriptures that though a mother may forget her sucking child, yet will He never forget us; He has adopted me in JESUS CHRIST, His only Son, in order to make me co-heir with that Son in the heavenly inheritance, and to share His own beatitude with me for ever. I think of these things, and then consider the wonderful economy of His fatherly love, the price paid by His Son to obtain this divine adoption for me, and the inestimable graces which accompanied and followed that merciful gift: and what can I withhold from such a Father, Whose only motive in all He asks of me, is the love He bears me, and the good He wills to bestow on me? I see nothing in His law but the sweetest and plainest of my duties:—love to Him; for love is the fulfilling of the law.

Therefore, I do not limit myself to the performance of those things which He commands under pain of His displeasure. I study what may please Him; the least sign He gives is a law to me; I refuse Him nothing, and complain of nothing; I gladly submit to all, even the most painful dispensations of His providence; for the name of Father always bids me look upon them as marks of His love, and trials of mine. So Job felt, when, in the depth of his afflictions He said: "Shall we receive good at the hand of GOD, and shall we not receive evil?" and, "Though He slay me, yet will I trust in Him." So far ought a Christian to carry His confidence and submission towards such a father as GOD.

How weak is human respect, when it attacks a heart full of filial love! The true child of GOD is inaccessible to the attractions and seductions of the world; he neither fears its threats nor its ridicule. He holds up his head, when His Father's honour is at stake, and declares his mind boldly. If he hides himself from the sight of men, he does so through humility, and never through weakness; he does nothing in order to be seen, but he does not trouble himself whether he is seen or not, whether he is praised or blamed, esteemed or contemned. To him, the world is as though it were not; abroad or alone, his eyes are always fixed on his Father, and he is taken up with Him alone.

How indeed should he trouble himself about pleasing the world, when he does not wish to please himself? He dreads nothing so much as self-contemplation: he avoids and forgets himself, and would shrink from diminishing His Father's glory in the slightest degree by any feeling of complacency; and if he ever surprises himself in doing so, he looks upon the fault as a crime.

The delicacy of his love goes further still. He is content to please God, without being eager to know whether he does please Him. He neglects no means whereby he may be acceptable in God's sight, but He asks for no sign or assurance that such is the case. His self-love might brood upon the gratifying knowledge, and so his love for God might lose in purity.

TWELFTH MAXIM.

Beware of resisting the leadings of grace: be thoroughly generous in great things and in small.

"*He that despiseth the day of small things shall fall by little and little.*"

XII.

OF FIDELITY.

It is the property of grace to strive against nature. Therefore we must expect that it will frequently, or rather continually, demand of us such things as are contrary to our vicious or imperfect inclinations; and that, consequently, nature will offer a violent resistance, and will not yield till the last moment. But the intention must always be on the side of grace. By the word intention, I do not mean fruitless desires, or constrained aversions, but a firm determinate resolution; not *I would*, but *I will:* triumphant over all likings and dislikings.

Such a generous intention, firmly resolved to follow out God's mind in all things, is not often met with, even among those who think they have wholly given themselves up to Him. In periods of sensible fervour, we declare ourselves ready and willing for everything; we fancy that our protestations spring from the depths of our will; but it is a mistake. They are only produced by the warmth of grace.

When that warmth has abated, and the soul is restored to itself and to ordinary grace, it is surprised to see that all its good resolutions have vanished. Or else, like S. Peter, we presume on our strength; and, so long as danger is afar off, we fancy ourselves ready to confront everything. But when the opportunity offers, we yield, as the apostle did, to the slightest temptation. There is a great difference, said a holy man who spoke from experience, between sacrificing one's life to GOD in a transport of devotion, and doing the same thing at the foot of the gallows. The true disposition of the will is to be judged of at the actual moment of the sacrifice, when the temporary action of the heavenly fire has ceased and the soul has cooled and returned to a state of unfelt grace.

Therefore we ought not lightly to imagine that we have this good will; on the contrary, we ought always to fear that we have it not. We are not indeed to be pusillanimous; but we are bound always to mistrust ourselves, and to rely only on help from heaven, surely trusting that it will not fail us in time of need. We are so weak, that we cannot be sure of victory beforehand; the slightest presumption renders us unworthy of it, and the enemy often snatches it from us when we had thought it all our own.

If we would fain never resist GOD, we must not lose sight of that saying of our LORD, "The spirit truly is willing, but the flesh is weak." We must watch and pray, as He bids us, that we may not enter into temptation. Watch, in order not to expose ourselves, and give advantage to the enemy; pray, in order to obtain from GOD that power which is wanting in ourselves. Thus abiding in the wholesome fear of being unfaithful to grace, GOD will preserve us from all evil; or if He sometimes suffers us to prove our own weakness, it will never be by a deadly fall: He will interpose His own hand between us and the blow, to prevent it from injuring us: He will raise us quickly, and we shall stand the more firmly afterwards.

The fear of resisting grace may be looked upon in yet another light. Such resistance is the greatest evil we have to dread. When GOD intends to take possession of a soul and rule it Himself, He gives it much instruction relative to its perfection; He watches with extreme attention over its thoughts, words, acts, and motives; overlooks nothing, examines every action, and keenly rebukes the slightest unfaithfulness.

Now, the soul cannot be too attentive to the light it thus receives from GOD, and His secret reproaches; and it is of the greatest importance to pay them fitting regard. For, in the first place, if we resist GOD's will, we arrest the course of our own perfection; we lay a stumbling-block across our road, and shall advance no further till we have surmounted it. Not only we shall not advance, but we shall fall back: for it is an axiom in the spiritual life, that whoso goes not forward falls backward. In the second place, graces hang on each other; one grace rightly used attracts a second; the second brings a third; and so on: and they form a chain which ends in holiness and final perseverance. In the same way, one grace rejected deprives us of the next, and so of those which would follow: and this may be carried so far, as to lead us to inevitable ruin.

Therefore it is always extremely dangerous to

break this chain; and as it is certain that we shall attain the full perfection which God requires of us, if we keep its links carefully united, so it is likewise certain that we shall fall away, and endanger our salvation, if we break that connection at any point whatever.

This is particularly true of certain principal graces which are, as it were, the great rings of the chain, and which involve consequences of extreme importance. Such are the grace of vocation, attraction to prayer, and others of that kind. They are, so to speak, the gate opening to the way by which God wills to bring us to the haven of salvation. If we correspond to them faithfully and constantly, we make our salvation sure; if we resist, we refuse the path which God points out to us, and which is perhaps the only one by which He intends to save us.

But it is right here to inform timid spirits that this chain is not broken by faults of inadvertence and impulse, or even of imprudence and indiscretion; in fact, it is not severed by sins of frailty, but by those committed knowingly and wilfully, and repeatedly. For God is not repelled by a first fault; He returns to the charge; His patience in waiting for a soul is long in proportion to the importance of the object; He does not withdraw altogether, till He perceives determinate obstinacy in the will.

He deals in like manner when He requires certain sacrifices. Sometimes He pursues a soul for whole years before He wearies, especially if the sacrifice is great, and the soul feels strong repugnance for it. But the moment when His pursuit ceases is known to Himself alone. Then such a soul drops out of the order of supernatural

Providence; it will probably never re-enter it, and its eternal salvation is at stake. GOD showed S. Theresa the place she would have had in hell, if she had lost that which was prepared for her in heaven. There was no medium for her; she must either have been a saint or a reprobate. How many souls are in this case without knowing it!

This is one of the chief reasons why masters of the spiritual life so strongly enforce the duty of recollectedness and correspondence to grace. Our LORD Himself teaches us that such attention and docility are the distinctive marks of His elect. "My sheep follow Me, for they know My voice." And it may be affirmed that the whole system of true direction consists in moulding souls to that disposition.

We ought to question GOD'S will in nothing, whether great or small. For it is not our place to decide on the greater or less importance of the things GOD requires of us, and we are very apt to run into error on such points. Besides, if GOD signifies His will concerning any matter, however small, that intimation at once invests it with importance: and, more than all else, we are bound to consider the intention and good pleasure of so great a Master. What, in itself, was the eating or the abstaining from a certain fruit? And yet the happiness of the human race depended on the observance of so apparently trifling a command. GOD is the absolute arbiter of the graces He bestows upon us, and also of the conditions to which He knits them. On our fidelity in a seemingly trivial matter, may depend the grace which He has prepared for us.

Opportunities of doing great things for GOD, are very rare; but those of doing little things arise continually; and refinement of love shows itself chiefly in careful diligence concerning these matters. Nothing proves the depth of our feelings towards GOD, and our desire of pleasing Him, more than the conviction that nothing is little in His service. And how, indeed, can we expect to be faithful to GOD in great things, if we are careless of obeying Him in small matters? These are more within our reach, more adapted to our weakness; those demand great exertion, such as is beyond our strength; and it would be presumptuous to suppose ourselves capable of them. Great acts of virtue are rather GOD's work than ours, and the lesser in some sort belong more to us, although GOD still has more to do with them than we have.

Faithfulness is not perfect, unless it embraces everything, without any exception. We ought to judge of the service due to GOD by that which we ourselves require of others. We expect it to be exact, punctual, and thorough; and we should take it much amiss if our servants declined to obey us, even in an inconsiderable matter. Is it too much, to serve GOD as we desire to be served ourselves?

The practice of little things keeps up our humility, and does not expose us to vanity. It is of inestimable value in the sight of GOD, if it proceeds from high motives. By its means we acquire that extreme purity of conscience which brings us so close to GOD. What, indeed, is the especial characteristic of His ineffable holiness? Its incompatibility with the slightest stain. And such, in proportion, is the holiness of the Saints.

How mistakenly do those persons act who reserve anything from GOD! who, so to speak, compound with Him; who consent to grant Him certain things, and obstinately refuse others; who watch themselves vigilantly on some points, and neglect themselves entirely respecting others; who set bounds to their perfection, and say in their hearts: So far will I go, and no farther. Do you not see that the very thing you withhold from GOD is that which He asks of you most emphatically, and concerning which He reproaches you most keenly and frequently? Then it is most important that you should yield it to Him; for if He presses you so strongly to do so, it is for your own interest, not for His. He sees better than you do, rather, He alone sees what is useful and necessary for your advance in holiness; and as He insists so much upon a certain point, it is a sure sign that that point is not so trifling as you think.

This is the great subject for self-examination, in which nothing must be overlooked. Let us search the inmost folds of our heart, and see whether there is any secret reservation, any robbery in our offering. And after all our investigations, let us pray GOD to bring His light into every dark corner of our souls, and make our inmost dispositions clear to ourselves; to suffer us not to wish to refuse Him the slightest thing; and to use His supreme authority in order to deprive us of that which we might have the weakness to hold back.

THIRTEENTH MAXIM.

Never dare to cease the struggle with that enemy who lives within the soul.

"*There is no discharge in that war.*"

XIII.

OF MORTIFICATION.

WHAT is that old man which S. Paul bids us crucify, and which CHRIST, in His own Person, bound to the tree of the Cross, to teach us what it deserves and how we ought to treat it? It is the flesh; or, in other words, it is everything within us that is opposed to the Spirit of GOD. This is the meaning of the Apostle, who, under the name of the flesh, comprises those vices which have the body for their object, and those also which originate in the mind. All the former pertain to sensuality, and all the latter to pride or inordinate self-esteem.

We must look back to original sin; and the two great wounds it inflicted on us, if we would rightly understand the nature of the war which Christians must wage with themselves, and of their two natures, spiritual and animal, whose inclinations are diametrically opposed to each other, and tend to mutual destruction. Thus we shall obtain a correct idea of Christian mortification; its necessity, extent, and continuity.

When Adam came from the hands of the Creator, his spirit was humble and subjected to God, and his body was docile and subjected to the spirit. So, all within him was in order, and he had only to keep it in the same state. Sin destroyed this order; Adam rebelled against God. His revolt arose from a principle of pride, and from a foolish hope of becoming like God if he ate the forbidden fruit. The rebellion of his flesh was destined to humble his pride, and to make him feel that the man, who, abusing his reason, aspires to equality with God, deserves the punishment of being set on a level with beasts, and subjected, like them, to the empire of the senses.

Therefore, the first thing he perceived after his sin, was this rebellion of the flesh; it was the indubitable sign and witness of his degradation; and, had he not been blinded by sin, that disorder, which he was ashamed to look upon, would have taught him how much more disgraceful and odious was the rebellion of his spirit against God. God must needs open his eyes, and enable him to judge of the exceeding disorder of his spirit, by the shame which he felt in consequence of the disorder of his flesh.

We, miserable children of Adam, are all born with a fatal inclination to this twofold disorder. The flesh disobeys the spirit; its appetites and motions forestal the will; the will is ready, first, to consent, then to excite, and lastly to enslave itself to them. Reason has the power of regulating the necessary appetites, as those of eating and drinking, and has absolute command over the others: but is weak enough to yield to them; and not only gratifies them frequently beyond necessity and contrary to the Creator's will, but degrades itself so low as to seek only the pleasure involved in the satisfaction of the senses, resting therein as its final end, using its ingenuity and powers to procure refined voluptuousness of all kinds, even to the overstepping the immutable bounds of nature, and yielding to excesses which nature's self abhors. A most humiliating state, which degrades man much below brute beasts, and which yet he feels so little, that he counts it a merit and a glory.

The disobedience of the spirit towards God goes, if possible, further still. We affect absolute independence; we consider liberty to consist in our doing whatever we please, without exception; and we look on this unlimited liberty as a right which cannot justly be disputed. We are annoyed by the sway God exercises over us, however necessary, mild, moderate, and favourable to our present well-being, and intending only our eternal happiness; lawful, reasonable, and wise. We are continually trying to shake off, or at any rate to weaken His yoke. Every law He lays down for us seems a blow aimed at our rights; every commandment is a burden to us; embargo laid on any matter is enough to make us desire it more vehemently. This strange disposition, which every one will find in himself if he will look deep enough, arises from a prodigious pride which knows no master, a mad idea of our own excellence, and a blindness respecting self which induces idolatry.

These are the diseases which the Gospel teaches us to understand and to cure. For the latter purpose it presents us with two kinds of mortifications. The aim of the first is to subjugate the body to the spirit; that of the second, to submit the spirit to GOD; in order so to restore primitive order and repair the evil caused by sin. They are respectively named exterior and interior.

The first degree of exterior mortification, which is absolutely binding on all Christians, is, to abstain from all pleasures forbidden by the law of GOD; to observe moderation in the use of those which are lawful; and religiously to observe the days of fasting and abstinence prescribed by the Church.

The second degree goes further. It refuses all unnecessary indulgence to the senses; it allows food only to hunger, drink to thirst, sleep to fatigue, clothes and lodging to necessity; and suffers nothing to flatter the taste, or favour effeminacy. All excessive care of the body foments its rebellion against the spirit; and experience teaches us that it is always ready to make an evil use of unnecessary indulgence. A mortified Christian leads an ordinary life, in no way singular, but simple, sober, and uniform, and strictly accordant to the rules of temperance and mortification. He looks on his body as a bad servant who obeys grudgingly, and is always endeavouring to shake off the yoke. Therefore he keeps it in strict dependence, and so subjects it to the spirit, that it not only does not hinder, but assists the spirit's operations. This is GOD'S law; reason alone would point it out; the Gospel only presses its observance on us, and makes that observance more easy.

The advantage of this moderate, but continual mortification is, that it gives no room for pride, is not in any way remarkable, and shields us from the excesses of indiscreet fervour. The flesh is mortified enough when it is reduced to mere necessaries, and deprived of all it may desire besides.

However (and this is the third degree of mortification), GOD sometimes inspires pious souls to perform afflictive penances; and these may be necessary, whether for the expiation of sin, or the quelling of pride, or the resisting of violent temptations. The rule is, that nothing of this kind be done, without the opinion or injunction of the confessor, and concerning this matter he ought to act with great discretion.

Because we read in the lives of some Saints, that they practised extraordinary austerities, our imagination is straightway heated, and we set about imitating them, with the idea that we cannot grow holy otherwise, but that then we shall infallibly do so. Wherein we are doubly mistaken; because, unless GOD asks these austerities at our hands, they are not necessary to our holiness; and, unless inspired and directed by grace, they may detract from it, instead of enhancing it. We ought to admire the acts of the Saints; to humble ourselves because we have neither their courage, nor their love of GOD; to be ashamed of doing so little in comparison with them; but, in this particular respect, we ought not to copy them, until GOD makes known to us (as He did to them) His will concerning it, and until that will is corroborated by him who stands in GOD'S place to us.

Mortification of the spirit brings the flesh into subjection much more efficaciously than any bodily austerity; and the reason of this is evident. The rebellion of the flesh against the spirit is, as I said before, the consequence and the punishment of the rebellion of the spirit against

God. Therefore, when we bend all our strength to subject our spirit to God, we immediately attack the principle of the disordered state of the flesh; and God, when He sees that the spirit is subjected to Him, remits the penalty due to its pride, and reduces the flesh to a state of duty. The more humble we are, the less we shall be exposed to the rebellion of the flesh.

Thus, then, interior mortification is incomparably the most necessary, because it touches the root and source of the evil. And what is to be mortified in the soul? Everything, without exception. All is infected by the poison of sin: passions, mind, will, yea, the very depth of the soul. Such is the war of man against himself, of grace against nature; and in this war he never may lay down his arms, because the enemy is never wholly conquered; and, cast down though he may be, the slightest negligence on our part will enable him to rise again.

As to the passions, in the first place. They are not essentially evil; but are simply the quick motions of the soul, whereby it tends to unite itself to good or to repel evil. Such they are according to God's primary institution and intention. But since the fall, the soul no longer knows either its true good or its true evil; it no longer considers the one or the other with reference to God, but only with reference to itself: it calls that good which flatters its pride and its self-love, or produces a momentary pleasure; it calls that evil which humbles and thwarts it, or interferes with the repose it seeks out of God and in created things. The passions are born of a blinded will, and guided by a darkened reason, therefore they misapprehend their object; they pursue it ardently, and because its falsity renders it unsatisfying, their craving increases more and more: ever disappointed, they ever seek a still eluding happiness. Except it be enlightened by the beams of grace, the soul continues in its state of delusion until death puts an end to all deception.

Thus the primary duty of a Christian is to deprive the passions of food, to check their impetuosity, quench their fire, and prevent their first emotions. To this end he must bring under control the senses which point out the object of passion, he must bridle the imagination which depicts it in seductive colours, and kindles desire, and he must curb every inordinate inclination. It is not enough to forbid indulgence in that which is manifestly criminal; those things must be cut off which are dangerous, doubtful, or in any degree apparently evil. The passions must even be deprived of things allowable and innocent, if clung to violently, for inordinate attachment is never harmless.

But such a war is not ended in a day: it must be carried on without a pause; no peace, no truce can be made with such dangerous enemies. Sometimes the passions appear to be dead, but they are only lulled: they wake as soon as vigilance ceases, and kindle in the heart a fresh and more mighty conflagration. Do not confine yourself to the passions; attack also affections that are simply natural, inclinations, repugnances—everything that clogs the heart, and does not leave it wholly free. Much more is involved than we think when we determine to search ourselves thoroughly, and to contend against every single thing within us that opposes the kingdom of grace.

For grace purposes nothing less than the destruction of the natural man, and the formation of the spiritual man. In whatever circumstances man ought to act by reason, the Christian ought to act on a principle supernatural and divine. S. Paul so decides: "Whether, therefore, ye eat or drink, or whatsoever ye do, do all to the glory of GOD." (1 Cor. xi. 31.) Judge from this precept how far you ought to carry inward mortification. Go on beyond natural affections. Be unsparing to sensitiveness, and that excessive captiousness by reason of which tears are always ready to flow, and one is vexed and annoyed by the most trivial word, the slightest contradiction, the least appearance of,—not to say contempt, but—coldness or indifference. Few are the Christians in whom all sensitiveness is mortified; who in the intercourse of life exact nothing, take exception at nothing, and do not even consider whether attention is paid to them or not. The complaint is made, and not unreasonably, that pious persons are more captious, harder to please, more easily offended, than are other men. For the honour of piety, and also for our own sakes, let us not give room for this reproach. Extreme sensitiveness is an unfailing source of trouble; it destroys peace of mind; we become suspicious of our neighbour; we look upon him with an evil eye; the outgoings of charity fail; and we run the risk of giving a fatal form to our feelings of resentment.

This is not enough. Even in the good you have in view, moderate the vivacity of desire, moderate eagerness, moderate activity. Study to attain continual self-possession. Rise above impatience: stop not merely its external signs, but stifle its inward movements so soon as they arise;

and as soon as you perceive them, prevent them from gaining the least sway over you. Complete possession of self, which is the work of grace, is the greatest blessing in life. It maintains inward peace, spiritual joy, evenness of soul; it edifies and wins our neighbour; dries up the source of many faults; and leaves us the free exercise of all our powers to perceive and perform successive duties as they come before us.

So much for the passions. As regards the understanding, how many things herein are to be mortified! It is filled from the first dawn of reason with prejudices contrary to the Gospel, respecting honour, riches, pleasures, and the customs of the world. Who does not look on his high birth as an absolute merit? What is it in GOD's sight? Nothing. What is it according to the standard of the Gospel? An obstacle to humility. Until your mind on this point is the mind of CHRIST, do not count yourself to be His disciple. Again, who is not ashamed of low birth, and sensitive to the thoughts and remarks of others on the subject? Reason tells us that this is folly, but will never raise us above it. The Gospel sets against these ideas the choice of our LORD Himself. He appeared on earth in the lowliest of conditions. He was born of the seed of David, the man after GOD's own heart; but waited till the royal family had sunk so low, that an artisan might be counted for His father; and yet how hard we find it to mould our mind in this respect to that of our LORD!

As much must be said of the preference given to a life of ease and comfort, rather than to one of labour and suffering.

How much prejudice exists on the subject of honour, deference, rank, and demeanour! Acquaintance with the false ideas prevalent on these points is equivalent to knowledge of the world. Did the primitive Christians live together on this wise? They acted as brethren, had one heart and one mind, held their love-feasts together, in honour preferred one another. What a forest of prejudices must be hewn down before we can attain to the exact practice of Christian morals, and hope to see all things in the same light in which our LORD Himself beholds them!

The destruction of these prejudices is not sufficient; their root dwells within ourselves, and we must turn our attention to that quarter; into that stronghold mortification must carry fire and sword. Where will you find the man who does not esteem himself beyond his deserts? Presuming on his own gifts and talents, and relying on his own judgment; jealous of the success of others professing the same calling, and unwilling to see them preferred to himself; dreading the shadow of contempt more than death, and acutely sensitive to the faintest whisper against his good fame?

Is this the mind of JESUS? His doctrine and His acts all preach humility, contempt and hatred of self. He willed to be despised and rejected of men; He suffered Himself to be crushed like a worm of the earth; He gave Himself up to humiliation, scorn, and infamy, even to the accursed death of the Cross. He wholly sacrificed His reputation, and yet, after man's judgment, how essential was its preservation, seeing that He came to be the Lawgiver, the Example, and the Saviour of the human race! By that sacrifice man was saved. This being so, dare we think highly of ourselves; believe in our own worth; labour to raise ourselves in the good opinion of others, or deceive ourselves so far as to believe that the glory of GOD is always concerned in the maintenance of our reputation? Shall we never think upon the truth that what JESUS our LORD was, He was in our stead, to teach us what we must be?

Now do you begin to perceive the full extent of inward mortification, and the series of long and painful struggles that you must undertake in order to be likened to your Head? Be not weary of learning your duties, nor terrified at their number or difficulty. Grace is all-powerful, and by its aid you will be more than conquerors.

Against your will the heaviest blows must be dealt: this is the dominant faculty of the soul, and the most corrupt, for in it sin takes its rise and attains to perfection. The understanding is often enlightened and convinced while the will resists and refuses to surrender. Attack it then, and determine on curbing its indocility. Deal with it so that it may grow yielding and obedient to GOD and man. It jealously asserts a right of liberty; this must not be permitted; the will must be bent by main force under the dispensations of Providence and the will of others. Suffer it not to incline to one thing rather than to another; train it to indifference, and let its rule be cheerfully to accept all vicissitudes great and small as they arise.

The will must die to its own likes and dislikes, must resist its inclinations and do violence to its aversions. It must study to cross itself in all things, and to quench its own desires. It must be willing to see hope disappointed, schemes brought to nought, purposes neglected or resisted. It must have no self-interest, and must learn never to consider self. It must enjoy divine consolations without becoming dependent on them: it must bear their removal without repining. It must receive crosses, and all manner of crosses, first uncomplainingly, then submissively, and at last joyfully. It must rise to the desire of never ceasing to bear the cross, taking no step, uttering no single word in order to free itself; lying in the Hands of GOD and of those, if any there be, who hold GOD'S place with regard to it, like wax which accepts the figure impressed on it; like water which has no form of its own and assumes that of the vessel in which it is placed. Its life, motion, and activity must only exist for the glory and the good pleasure of GOD.

Oh! death of the will, how difficult, how rare thou art! What Christian, nay, what Saint exists, who seeks nothing in and for himself? That is the height of perfection; but how few attain it! how few even profess to seek it!

The value of this death is equal to its difficulty and rarity. It sets us above the events and circumstances of life, health and sickness, riches and poverty, esteem and contempt, honours and humiliations, good report and evil report; above natural friendship and aversion; above the gifts of GOD and the withdrawal of His gifts; His marks of favour and His trials; above even the vicissitudes of the spiritual life. We are hereby enabled to cling only to the will of GOD, loving, resting, and trusting in nothing beside, and thus partaking of its holiness and changelessness.

I shall say nothing of what I called the mortification of the very depth of the soul. This is not within our scope, nor within that of ordinary grace. This is the work of GOD alone, in those whom He vouchsafes to bring through the terrible trials that lead to this death.

Such is the lot of very few persons, and those who are not called to it would vainly attempt to understand its nature.

Have I opened a sufficiently wide field for Christian conflict? Have I given some idea of the war to be waged against self, the courage, patience, and endurance necessary in order to enter upon it, to maintain it, and to reach full and perfect victory? Do you now know what is that old man on whose fall the new man is to rise?

FOURTEENTH MAXIM.

When God bids thee be still in prayer, humble thyself silently before His Majesty.

"*Be still, and know that I am God.*"

XIV.

OF CONTEMPLATIVE PRAYER.

It is well known that there are two kinds of mental prayer, Meditation and Contemplation. Meditation is to contemplation what active recollectedness is to passive. In meditation, all the powers of the soul, memory, understanding, will, and even imagination, have free scope, and from each is drawn what is most suitable to the end in view. A distinct subject is presented before the mind, on which reflections are made: affections are thence drawn out, and resolutions are formed. There are many good books on this matter, and I shall here say little respecting it.

In contemplation, or prayer properly so called, the soul neither reflects nor forms affections and resolutions. Yet neither the understanding nor the will are idle. For if the contemplation be distinct, the understanding sees, though without any chain of reasoning, the object presented to it by God. If it be confused, and do not offer to the soul any special object, the understanding sedulously holds itself in the presence of God, humbles itself before His Supreme Majesty, and listens silently to the instructions given without sound or distinctness of words, which is the manner in which GOD's instructions are commonly given. This attention is itself an act of the understanding, unperceived because so simple, but not therefore the less real. The confused, general, indistinct object, which is then present to the soul, is GOD Himself, wrapped in the cloud of faith; whilst in distinct contemplation GOD sets forth some one of His perfections, or some particular mystery of religion.

We may form some idea of these two sorts of contemplation, if we remember the different ways in which we look at things about us, sometimes fixing our eyes on one certain point, but sometimes looking vaguely, and attracted by nothing in particular.

Nor is the repose of the will in contemplation to be considered as inaction. For, in the first place, its freedom is continually exercised, because we are at prayer only because we choose to be so, and frequently have to resist the temptation of giving it up on account of distractions, dryness, or even of evil thoughts which assail us at such times. Secondly, the will is either in a state of union, or constant tendency to union, with GOD, as it practises this exercise with the one object of being united to Him. In the third place, when it receives a sense of Divine sweetness, peace and joy are shed abroad upon it, and are gladly accepted. Lastly, if the soul receives nothing, and the time of prayer is a time of suffering, the will is then in a state of sacrifice, accepted in submission to GOD's good pleasure. In that true rest bestowed by GOD upon the soul, as in the false rest which is the result of illusion, there is always some action on the part of the understanding and of the will; and the difference between real and illusive repose is, not that the soul acts in true prayer and is silent in false, but that in the former God is the agent, while fancy or Satan acts in the second. However it may be, for I do not wish to go to the bottom of this matter, it would be wrong to give the name of idleness to the holy repose in which God holds the soul during contemplation: and no one should be obliged on that account to give it up. But what ought to be done is this, to examine by the rules laid down by the Saints whether or not this repose comes from God. If it does, who shall be rash enough to dare disturb the peace of a soul in which God is working? If it does not, the soul must be undeceived and set right.

These rules are as follow. In the first place, so long as we have the free use of our powers, and can meditate with ease, we ought not to leave off. But it is the advice of spiritual writers, that when we have sufficiently imbibed the truths under meditation, and have investigated them under every phase, we should wholly or partly cease from acts of the understanding, and pass on to those of the will, which are much more essential, and lead it to love the truths it has already learned. For the aim of meditation is to move the will, and rouse it to avoid vice and practise virtue.

Secondly, after meditation has been practised for some time, and the proper fruit has been derived thence, it sometimes appears that God is drawing the will to a peculiar state of rest; it now produces no distinct affections, or, if it desires to do so through long habit, it is gently checked and drawn to enjoy rather than to act.

Then the soul is entering upon the passive way. GOD Himself is leading it, and it would hinder its own advancement if it offered any resistance.

Thirdly, it is sometimes the case that a person truly devoted to GOD, finds his efforts to meditate all in vain: and if after many attempts he is absolutely unable to succeed, whether by reason of a simple character of mind which grasps a subject at a single glance, or lightness and vivacity of imagination, or any other cause, he will do well, with his director's consent, to try simply to remain quiet in the presence of GOD, entreating the HOLY SPIRIT to teach him to pray, listening like Samuel and David to hear the LORD speak to his heart. And if this method suits him: if he feels calm and peaceful, and after such prayer loves GOD's service more dearly, and sets himself to his daily conflicts more bravely, there is no doubt that his prayer is good, and that GOD is acting in it: the fact is guaranteed by the effects, which are peace, spiritual joy, love of GOD, and an effectual desire of advancement in holiness, which are so many fruits of the HOLY SPIRIT.

Fourthly, it may occur that when we betake ourselves to our prayers we feel our powers fettered, so that we cannot bring them to bear on the subject proposed for meditation; we may take up a book, such as the Imitation, or one of similar character, but so soon as we lay it down we entirely lose recollection of what we have been reading, and thus the mind remains, as it were, in empty space. If this impotence is accompanied by a sweet peace, which fully occupies the soul, we may certainly believe that GOD is placing the soul in a state of passive prayer, and we must beware of making any effort to withdraw from that way. Even if this impotence be accompanied by perplexity, darkness, and temptation, yet if the soul is true and stands firm against these tempests, they will soon be followed by a great calm, and may be regarded as a preparation for the most signal favours of GOD.

In the last place, the usual proof of the goodness of prayer, is the generous and constant practice of interior mortification. There is no cause for apprehension concerning the prayer of a person who is single-hearted, straightforward, teachable, humble, capable of great self-control, endued with a good will, cheerfully undertaking every means suggested for overcoming faults, acknowledging them frankly, and taking rebukes in good part. If the spirit of GOD guides the rest of his conduct, will it forsake him at the time of prayer? We cannot suppose this possible.

But the application of these rules belongs to the director. We should not judge ourselves, else we should run the risk of self-deception. Humility and obedience are the two points on which the interior life turns; therefore, when we believe it to be GOD's will that we should leave the ordinary way, we should candidly represent our state to our spiritual guide, and thus enable him to decide. This is the more necessary, because without his advice we cannot maintain ourselves in the different states of prayer, and we ought to keep him informed of all that takes place in our souls, in order that he may shield us from delusion, and strengthen us against temptations and trials. If, through lack of knowledge, or prejudice against contemplative prayer, the director should decide mistakenly concerning our state, we ought at once to acquiesce in his decision, and do as he desires. Thus S. Theresa abstained one whole year from contemplation, by order of her confessor. Yet we should feel a discomfort, an inward constraint, which would be a certain sign that he is removing us from our proper position, and making us resist the workings of God. Then we might consult other persons more enlightened, and follow their advice. Thus, again, the same Saint, whose contemplation was condemned by the doctors of Alcala, was reassured by S. Peter of Alcantara and S. Francis Borgia. God always blesses obedience and submission of the judgment. He will, in His own way, cause the confessor to see our state in its true light, or else He will direct us to some other person. God alone can and may bid the reason to be silent in time of prayer. He endowed the soul with powers, in order that they might be used so long as He grants free disposal of them, and it is a false and heretical doctrine of Molinos, that man ought to annihilate them himself, may reduce them, that is, to inaction. Inaction, thus produced, would render us a prey to every freak of the imagination, and every delusion of the heart.

Besides, according to the principles of true philosophy, the soul cannot of itself trammel its powers; this act necessitates a superior agent, distinct from itself, and acting upon it with irresistible force. For when God has so bound the soul, it is startled by the power exercised on it, perceives clearly that the force is from without, and sometimes, but always vainly, offers extreme resistance. So also when one who knows this state speaks of it, he says, that no effort will enable him to use his memory, he cannot reflect, nor waken any emotion, he must needs be, as GOD's Word hath it, even as it were a beast before Him, as a log of wood which must wait till the Hand of GOD shall kindle it. These are usual expressions on the part of persons thus exercised; they do not place themselves in that state; such an assertion is a contradiction. Moreover, when sensible tokens of grace are withdrawn, which frequently happens, this state is far from giving pleasure to the soul; it is, on the contrary, very painful, being absolutely counter to nature. We can only continue in this condition by reason of fidelity, because we cannot doubt GOD's will concerning it. If we listened to our own promptings we should renounce contemplation.

A confessor who is not on his guard may be deceived, and may lend an ear to the description of fictitious states of the soul. But if he knows what contemplation is, and if nothing is disguised, he cannot possibly confound real impotence with that state of inaction to which a person may bring his own self.

Let it not be supposed that true contemplation is an act which, being once entered on, continues naturally and needs no renewal. This error, if taught by any mystic, lapses into the heresy of Molinos. I say, *if* taught, for it may well have happened that those who have thought so may have made a mistake, and have taken for the description of contemplation, that of the act by which the soul gives itself to GOD, and consecrates itself to His service in order to fulfil His will in all things. This latter act has no need of renewal so long as we are faithful to it, for it always subsists in intent and in deed. But yet it is not a continuous act which nothing suspends or interrupts; it is an act transient in itself, but abiding in its effects so long as it is not annulled by renunciation. If I have formed the purpose of making a journey, and have set out on the road, there is no need that I should continually renew my intention, so long as I advance towards my journey's end without stopping on my way, or turning aside from it.

FIFTEENTH MAXIM.

Cling not to sensible sweetness, and suffer dryness with a good heart.

"*Though He slay me, yet will I trust in Him.*"

XV.

OF DIFFICULTIES IN PRAYER.

THIS maxim refers to contemplative prayer, and to the manner in which they should act who practise it. Its beginnings are generally very sweet. GOD gives the soul a sense of what He is; He pours out His graces; He brings us into His banqueting-house, and His banner over us is love. Here is a paradise of delights of which we had no conception; here we breathe afresh: here we delight in liberty till then unknown. The heart is too narrow to contain the blessings lavished upon it. When alone, we relieve ourselves by sighs and tears. This state lasts for a time. The Bridegroom indeed hides Himself at intervals in order to be more keenly desired. But the soul calls Him back eagerly, seeks Him uneasily, speedily finds Him, and derives fresh comfort from His return.

When GOD gives the soul a foretaste of those pure deep joys of which He is the only source, He does so in order to inspire it with aversion and contempt for the false pleasures incident to the enjoyment of created things. Experience is a more efficacious teacher than theory. But what then? That wretched self-love, which dwells within our hearts, makes an ill use of GOD'S favours. Hardly has it tasted them, when it seeks them eagerly, gloats over them with unacknowledged complacency, persuades the soul to make them the motive and end of its prayers, good works, and contests with self; so that heavenly pleasures are sought for as ardently as the voluptuous seek the gratifications of the world; and by means of a selfish and mercenary spirit, GOD is loved only for the pledges of His love.

Yet these persons think that they love GOD with ardent love for His own sake. But it is a mistake; in truth, selfish gratification is the object that is beloved; and this is proved by the fact, that as soon as no sensible pleasure is to be found in intercourse with GOD, the soul becomes uneasy, agitated, despondent, or despairing, and sometimes forsakes everything, and reproaches GOD with having forsaken it in the first place.

Not thus does GOD will to be loved and served. In order to attract and win the soul, He vouchsafes to give it some slight foretastes of its promised happiness, but will not allow us to cling to them, nor to make them our motive and aim. Certainly man is born for happiness, but its enjoyment is reserved for the next life; this life is the season for trial and for acquiring merit. GOD only prepares crosses for His friends on earth, and, in order to dispose them for receiving such from His hand, He begins by rendering that hand dear to them on account of the blessings it sheds upon them. In proportion as these sweet blessings are delightful and absorbing, we must expect the following crosses to be rough and overwhelming. I would therefore say to those whose state I am describing: gratefully receive these first favours; fear not to enjoy them simply; they are "milk for babes," food suitable to weakness. If a director sought to deprive you of them, and ordered you to give them up, he would take away your necessary support and deprive you of the heavenly dew which is required by your soul in its present state. But then you ought skilfully to profit by the short occasional hidings of GOD'S face, in order to persuade you to bear such privations quietly: the Bridegroom will return, but you must learn to wait quietly for His own time, and not attempt to regulate it according to your impatience: let Him open your eyes gradually to the meanness of self-love, inspire you with generous disinterestedness, and lead you to feel that He is infinitely beyond His gifts, that He ought to be loved for His own sake, and that His will, and the fulfilment of His will, are the paramount objects of His servants.

Thus a spirit of detachment will gradually be formed in your minds, and you will be prepared to accept, without terror or danger, the time of weaning from sensible sweetness, when GOD is about to give you more solid nourishment in the exercise of bare faith.

By bare faith, I mean that state in which we serve GOD without any pledge or assurance of acceptance. This state is extremely painful to self-love; and so it must be, because it is intended to undermine it imperceptibly, and at last to destroy it as far as is possible in this life. If we entered suddenly and unpreparedly on a state so crucifying to nature, we should soon be repelled and give up all idea of leading an interior life. Therefore GOD with infinite wisdom provides for the difficulties of the advance: He does not wean the soul until it has attained a certain growth, and although He may afterwards keep it in a habitual state of privation, He yet tempers its rigour by frequent tokens of His love. The soul, on its side, long remembers the first graces bestowed on it by GOD, and this remembrance serves as a support in times of destitution. Besides, this state of bare faith has its degrees, the last of which is not reached till after the lapse of many years.

Yet, in spite of this wise economy of grace, few persons overcome these first difficulties. Most are so soft, sensual, and self-seeking, that they cannot resolve to give up the happiness of the infancy of their spiritual life. They do their utmost to retain it, and when deprived of it for a length of time, they think that all is lost. But GOD disregards their alarms; when once He has withdrawn these sweetnesses, He restores them but temporarily and at long intervals, and appears chary of them in proportion to the eagerness with which they are desired.

Most persons therefore, seeing that these privations last longer than they like, lose hope, give up the practice of contemplative prayer, under the plea that the attempt is mere waste of time; they grow unwatchful, allow their minds to become distracted, and, despising their Creator, turn back to created things. It is well if they fall not even below what they were when GOD took them in hand, but merely resume the former practices which they ceased in order to follow the leadings of grace. For they commonly become worse than they were before, either as a punishment from GOD or in consequence of their own secret vexation, pride, and despondency. They not only give up the interior life, but sometimes relinquish pious exercises altogether; the senses and passions resume their sway; less strength is forthcoming to resist them. Those who knew such persons in their time of fervour are startled and scandalized by these falls, which are unjustly attributed to the practice of contemplative prayer, as if it were responsible for the errors consequent upon giving it up. The salvation of these persons runs most imminent risks.

Therefore it is important, that those who are called by GOD to an interior life, should know that bare faith is, strictly speaking, the essence of that life; the pleasant state in which they are first placed, is only the prelude and preparation for it. This bare faith glorifies GOD most, because He is hereby served in a manner worthy of Himself, which yields no pleasure to self-love, and wherein we in no wise seek ourselves, but practise self-forgetfulness and self-sacrifice, and give ourselves over to bear all such rigour as it shall please a merciful justice to exercise upon us. If, as S. Paul teaches, the elect are those whom GOD has predestined to be conformed to the image of His Son: if their holiness increases in proportion to such conformity; if the interior life is that which most resembles the Divine Pattern; then those who by GOD's special favour are intended for this life, must expect that, while on earth, He will treat them as He treated His only Son, on account of the great scope of His designs regarding them, the glory He intends to derive from them, and that other glory wherewith He wills to crown them.

Therefore the sweet peace of a happy prayer will be succeeded by long periods of distaste, dryness, or weariness, which will render the exercise of prayer as painful as it was pleasant in times past. Perplexity, darkness, and terror, will take the place of light, joy, and confidence. We shall feel ourselves the sport of temptations with regard to purity, faith, or hope. We shall continually fancy that we have yielded, and no power will avail to assure us of the contrary. Thus we must long go on blindly, led by obedience, hoping against hope, loving God without knowing that we love Him or are loved by Him, but feeling ourselves rather the objects of His displeasure; and not till we have passed through utter darkness, shall we find ourselves born again to a new life which will be the precious pledge of our eternal happiness.

All interior souls do not pass through trials of the same length, or involving equal suffering. God regulates the measure for each as He wills; but all do go through trials; all pledge themselves to do so, and long for them more than they dread them; fear belongs to their nature only, but desire is in their will. For the love of crosses is one of the first feelings that God implants in their hearts, and that love is always on the increase.

You then, who are entering on this state of bare faith, must gird yourself up bravely to endure the first occasions of your Lord's absence, so as to win His own support when you are suffering under the weight of His rigour. Be sure that, if you are faithful, He will lead you as far as you can go, and will lay more crosses upon you than you will ask for. He tries those severely who love Him, in order that they may love Him more. But at the same time He communicates to them an unseen strength. It is scarcely credible, though certain, that, in proportion to their suffering, their souls enjoy a peace which passeth all understanding. Besides imparting support, GOD inspires them with words which have power to support other souls weaker than their own; as S. Paul bears witness: "Who comforteth us in all our tribulations, that we may be able to comfort them which are in any trouble."

Do you dread trials? They are indispensably necessary for your admission to heaven. The willing acceptance of them will make them sweet. You do not appreciate the all-powerful operation of grace, and the wondrous changes which it brings to pass in the mind and heart. Yield yourself up to it, and have no uneasiness concerning your own infirmity. You will be weak only so far as you rely on yourself; but if you place your whole confidence in GOD, you will be able to say with S. Paul: "I can do all things through CHRIST Which strengtheneth me."

You may ask me: Why must we bear so many internal and external trials? Can we acquire holiness at no less price? No; the Gospel affirms that holiness is only to be attained by suffering, or at least by the will to suffer. Holiness consists in readiness to embrace all the crosses that it may please GOD to send us. GOD does not bid us to forestal crosses, but it is His will that we should stand firm to receive them, and that when they are laid upon us we should accept them bravely. He who shrinks away will never be holy.

Do you say: At this cost I will consent never to be holy, provided I can be saved? Fool! you open your eyes only to the fleeting ills of this life, and close them to the exceeding weight of glory and happiness which awaits you! Niggard! you would buy heaven at the lowest possible price, fearing to pay too highly for it! Base and sordid soul! you consider only your own gain, and would do nothing for GOD! See what your salvation has cost your Lord JESUS CHRIST, and complain, if you dare, of what it costs yourself. All you ask is bare salvation; but how can you count even on that, if you refuse to be made holy? How can you be sure that you will do enough, and no more than enough, to assure your salvation? Ought you not rather to fear doing too little than too much?

Besides, supposing that you should attain salvation, shall you escape suffering? Is there no purgatory? And for whom is it reserved, if not for you? Shall you go to heaven without the purification of that fire which must consume all that remains in you of self-love? I cannot insist too much on this point, because to the eyes of faith it is conclusive.

I have a few more words to say on the subject of dryness. Those who suffer from it are very subject to distracted thoughts; indeed they are inevitable, and they torture many good souls who fancy them wilful, and yet cannot defend themselves from their attacks, however strenuous their efforts may be. For the comfort of such persons, I would beg them to notice, that no distraction of thought is sinful unless it arises in the will, and is fostered in the heart. We are not distracted at prayer, if, contrary to our will, the mind admits a different object to that on which we wish to dwell. We go to prayer, intending to worship GOD and unite ourselves to Him, when the imagination suddenly strays off to a multitude of different subjects. If we feel this to be troublesome and unpleasant, and if, as soon as we perceive it, we quietly recal our thoughts to the subject of our prayer, or to the simple contemplation of GOD, then we are not distracted in will, because our intention of prayer and union with GOD remains unbroken; and even if such distractions should last during the whole time of prayer, it would be none the worse for them.

We are not responsible for the thoughts which enter our minds, but it depends on our own will whether we entertain them or not, and also on the general disposition of our minds at other times. If we grant too much freedom to the fancy and senses, if we allow the mind to be excited by all sorts of subjects, if we waste our energies by the exercise of foolish curiosity or by frivolous conversation and idle thoughts, and if we are not careful to keep our heart free from all desires and undue attachments, it is not surprising that at the time of prayer we should find a habit of recollection difficult to acquire, and that we are then disturbed by those things to which we usually devote our time. For such distractions we are responsible, even if, at the moment, we yield no consent to them; because we have drawn them upon ourselves.

But if, in the course of the day, we keep a curb on our fancy and our senses, if we are only attentive to the duties of our position, if we suffer nothing to divert us from the sense of GOD's presence which ought to occupy our heart: then we may disregard all distractions that intrude upon our prayers, provided we do not consent to them. Moreover, it may be assumed that we do not consent to them in any wise, if we live in a state of habitual recollection. These rules are simple and adapted to set aside scruples with regard to attention at prayer, whether it be vocal or mental.

Usually we bring to our prayers the same state of mind in which we are accustomed to live. GOD will not work a miracle to keep us recollected then; and we shall vainly endeavour ourselves to be so, if at other times we suffer our mind and heart to wander at their will.

With regard to souls raised by GOD to a state of passive prayer, and in a state of dryness, some points should be observed. First, that in this state it is impossible to secure freedom from the vagaries of the imagination. GOD inspires no thought on holy subjects, and kindles no feeling in the heart; therefore the soul feels, as it were, cast into space, and the imagination takes free wing. But if we take good heed, we shall see that our wandering thoughts are vague and unconnected; they do not touch the will, they leave no trace behind them; so that afterwards we should find it very difficult to recal them, which is a plain sign that we did not intentionally allow our minds to dwell on them.

In the second place, these distractions, far from being hurtful, are useful to the soul, because they try it and accustom it both to feel its own misery and to bear it patiently. It is very painful for a pious soul to become the sport of imagination and its follies; it is distressing to lose our recollectedness and to think vain thoughts during prayer; but these things humble us, by teaching us what we are, and proving that our own endeavours cannot obtain us one good thought or feeling. Self-love steals in everywhere. If we feel any sensible emotions during prayer or communion, we are apt to grow self-complacent, to rest on them, and so defile the purity of our intention. In a state of dryness, self-love has no support, and is therefore startled and hurt. But we must despise its complaints and grumblings, and the false reasonings whereby it endeavours to perplex us. The proof that this aridity is profitable to our spiritual advancement is, that under its action nature suffers, and is gradually consumed and destroyed, while the life of grace spreads and gains strength.

In the third place, these distractions form a part of God's design. He makes use of them to hide His workings from the soul, which is thus deterred from self-contemplation. When it enjoys a state of peace and calmness, it is sure to dwell upon it with feelings of too strong attachment and pleasure; and this is not pleasing in God's sight; therefore He gradually removes all that induces this condition, and allows the soul to become apparently a prey to distractions, while He works within it hiddenly and unknown.

Beware then of losing patience or hope when imagination thus runs wild. Do not suppose that your prayer is worse or less pleasing to God. Do not listen to self and Satan, who would induce you to give it up as waste of time. Do not take up a book for the purpose of occupying your mind. Directors should never recommend such a practice to souls in this state; it would be leading them back to meditation from which God calls them to cease. Neither should you strain yourself or weary mind and body to repel these distractions: such efforts are useless; far from calming the imagination they do but irritate and excite it the more, as flies perpetually driven away do but return more obstinately. Despise these things; leave them to drop naturally, without exciting yourself to beat them down; content yourself with mentioning them to your confessor; do not speak of them as sins, and do not labour to find out whether you have consented to them.

If thus you keep your mind at rest in times of mere distraction, you will have grace to do the same in the midst of temptations, when GOD allows them to besiege the soul and to assault it violently in time of prayer, which is the time generally chosen by the devil for this purpose. If you act as I have just advised (for the rules concerning temptations and distractions are nearly identical) you have nothing to fear; the devil will be beaten; his attempts to turn you out of the right way will only cause you to cleave to it more truly, and to advance in it more surely. But the matter of temptations deserves a separate maxim and explanation.

SIXTEENTH MAXIM.

The tempter blends cunning and violence; we must meet him with prayer and watchfulness.

"*The battle is not yours, but God's.*"

XVI.

OF TEMPTATIONS.

THE devil has little hold upon souls which devote themselves to prayer and mortification. Common temptations do not concern them, because they allow them no entrance; if they happen to be occasionally surprised by them, it is a matter of little moment, and has no evil consequences. Moreover, the devil does not generally originate these temptations: "But every one," says S. James, "is tempted when he is drawn away of his own lust and enticed." Therefore such souls are usually exposed to such temptations only as GOD permits to exercise their patience, deepen their humility, increase their merit, and add brightness to their crown. Of these temptations only I am about to speak.

In the first place, I think that they are too greatly dreaded. It would be presumptuous to defy the devil, but it is weak to be afraid of him. As S. Augustine says, he is a chained dog, who can bark and tease, but cannot bite if we keep out of his reach. Such strong apprehension may arise from many different causes. The imagination often has much to do with it. Struck, in reading the biographies of some Saints, by the account of temptations to which they are said to have been subjected, a fanciful person imagines himself about to pass through the same phases, and, like them, to be driven to extremities. Take comfort, timid soul! great temptations are intended only for brave hearts. Be not vain enough to suppose that GOD will deal with you as He has dealt with certain, among His elect, whose number is very small.

In some cases, this fear arises from a faint and craven spirit. Such hearts are narrow, ungenerous, incapable of great sacrifices; they shudder at the least danger; if piety is to suit them, it must be moderate, easy, tranquil, sheltered from storm or tempest. No sooner do the winds blow, and the skies gather blackness, and the thunders roll, than they think the whole spiritual house is about to fall. Coward soldiers! you would fain conquer without fighting; victory is theirs only who resist unto blood; but the mere sight of the enemy puts you to flight.

So, too, this fear springs from want of confidence in GOD. If we felt Him to be all our strength we could not be overcome; for what has he to fear who has GOD ALMIGHTY on his side? "The LORD is my light and my salvation, whom then shall I fear? The LORD is the strength of my life, of whom then shall I be afraid? Though an host of men were laid against me, yet shall not my heart be afraid; and though there rose up war against me, yet will I put my trust in Him."

But, instead of looking to the LORD, we look

only to self, measuring our strength against that of Satan; and, as we see that we are but weakness, we lay down our arms and turn our back before the battle begins. We pretend that this is humility and just distrust of self. Not at all; it is self-love and presumption, which professes that success depends only on our courage, instead of awaiting it from GOD alone. In our blindness, we do not consider that the due time of GOD'S help is the very time of contest; that before that time it would be useless and dangerous to think ourselves strong, as S. Peter did; but that when the time has come, GOD will help us, and will do so the more, the more we put our trust in Him.

And why should we fear temptations? Do we not know them to be necessary for us, because without them we can make no progress in the way of perfection? Yes: they are necessary to strengthen us in the very virtues which they assail. Never will you reach a high degree in purity, faith, hope, or love of GOD and of your neighbour, unless you are strongly tempted with regard to these virtues. Our LORD teaches us that storms prove the stability of the house; the temptations by which the devil seeks to rob us of our virtues, render those virtues dearer to us; constrain us to greater efforts for their retention, and quicken and multiply our prayers that it may please GOD to save us from suffering the loss of them.

Trials are necessary to self-knowledge. "He that hath no experience, knoweth little," saith the son of Sirach. We must have faced the enemy, and that more than once: we must have often known ourselves in danger of falling: in order truly to appreciate that we can do nothing without God, and can do all things through Him. Before the contest we are either cowardly or presumptuous; only in the very time of the struggle we learn to judge ourselves rightly. If conquered, defeat brings humility; if, despite all resistance and foresight, we are on the point of perishing, we feel the greater need of crying to God for help; if, just when we give ourselves up for lost, God suddenly delivers us from danger, the very risk we have run forces us to feel that it is to Him we owe the victory.

Trials are necessary to make us put aside all self-confidence. When the violence of temptation is extreme: when strength is exhausted through long resistance: when we know not whither or how to escape, and nothing seems left but surrender: then, giving up all hope in self, and having nothing more we can do in our own defence, we must needs cast ourselves into the arms of God. This is the moment for which God is ever on the watch; now we shall be most certain to receive His help. He shows us how inevitably we are about to fall, in order that we may grasp the conviction that He alone can hold us back on the brink of the precipice, can stay our fall and lift us up, when to all appearance we really have fallen. He loves to bring us up from the gates of death, as it is written: "The Lord killeth and maketh alive; He bringeth down to the grave and bringeth up."

In the last place, trials are necessary to bring us into closer union with God. When do we call on Him more fervently than when "our feet are almost gone, and our treadings have well-nigh slipt?" When do we hide in His bosom, if not when the enemy threatens to deprive us of the life of grace? In a state of apparent safety we forget to think of GOD; temptation calls us back to Him and binds us to Him indissolubly.

As for those whom GOD intends for the guidance of others, temptations are essential to them. There is no better teacher than experience. Knowledge of temptation teaches them to feel more compassion for those who are tempted, and to attend to them with more charity. They understand the tactics of the devil; they neither dread his deceits nor his open attacks; they know with what weapons to oppose him, and how to prevent and frustrate his plans. They are in a position to encourage others, and to give them profitable advice. A director who has not passed through similar trials has not the same advantage. He is timid, hesitating, and uncertain how to decide; he bewilders those who apply to him, or, what is worse still, he misunderstands their condition and judges them harshly; he mistakes the manner of dealing with them, repels them, and drives them to despair.

You fear temptations, but "GOD is faithful Who will not suffer you to be tempted above that ye are able; but will with the temptation also make a way to escape, that ye may be able to bear it."

Let us reflect on these words.

GOD is faithful. His promises fail not. It is His will that His children's love should be tried. He permits the devil to assail them. But still the promise of His help stands firm. How can hell itself avail to hurt us, if GOD is on our side? In time of need let us turn confidently to Him. We must not be ready to forsake Him, and then He will never forsake us. The devil's intention is to injure and ruin us; the intention of GOD is to strengthen our virtue, and save us by those very things in which He allows him to tempt us. Satan can do nothing of himself, and if we give him no opportunity for tempting us, he will only do so by GOD's permission, and must keep within its limits. But GOD will not suffer you to be tempted above that ye are able. His justice, His faithfulness, His loving-kindness forbid His doing so. Therefore, before He allows temptations to assail us, He waits till our virtues have attained some degree of strength.

He does not bring us face to face with our enemies at the beginning of our course, when we are still timid and tottering, easily startled, and ready to fall. But He prepares us for the strife, and renders us strong and fit for war before He brings us into the presence of the enemy.

Besides this, He gives us present help always in proportion to the attack: He is beside us, He inspirits us to fight, and moreover fights with us. The grace we then receive is always such as to render us superior to our enemies, and is sufficient to ensure victory.

Let me add, that so great is the goodness as well as the power of GOD, that He wills to make our very falls turn to our spiritual advantage, provided that we turn to Him with that hearty and loving penitence to which He calls us by the strongest pleadings and most urgent motives. Thus, even the falls of David and S. Peter, being turned to good account, contributed to their sanctification.

Why then need you fear temptations, if your trust in GOD is such as it ought to be? You complain that they beset you during prayer and Holy Communion, and that the devil chooses these very times to attack you. Say rather, that GOD chooses for your exposure to temptation, the period when you are best prepared to resist evil; when your immediate intention is to unite yourself to Him, when CHRIST, present in your heart, will Himself repel the assaults of the enemy.

"But this deprives me of peace in prayer!" Very probably your soul may then be stirred and troubled on the surface; but it depends on yourself whether its depths are calm. It is not in the devil's power to touch that depth of the soul, which is the true seat of peace. You lose the sense of calmness, but that does you no harm; you may, if you choose, retain the reality.

"But it debars me from Holy Communion!" By no means. You have only a more urgent reason for partaking of it. The devil insinuates the feeling which keeps you away, only because he knows what strength you obtain from it, and how certain is his defeat, if you meet him in that strength. In fact, the most violent temptations subside and fade away, the moment we receive the adorable Body of CHRIST. I do not know that it ever happened that immediately after Holy Communion any soul, tormented by frightful thoughts till then, did not find itself relieved from them.

"But the devil suggests pictures, thoughts, desires, that fill my mind with horror!" So much the better, if his suggestions do fill your mind with horror; for it is a manifest proof that you reject them, and that GOD rejects them in you. Do you know that our LORD said, "Out of the heart proceed evil thoughts;" that is to say, our thoughts are not evil, except in so far as the heart conceives and encourages them? How then should those thoughts be evil, which your heart detests? Sin lies, not in having the object present to the mind, or impressed upon it, but in the consent given by the will; and nothing is more contrary to this consent than the state of mind in which you are.

"But I seem to have no strength whatever to resist such temptations!" Since they fill you with horror, and you would rather die than encourage them, you do resist, and that with all the force of your will. It may well be that you do not perceive this force; but it is none the less, nor the less active; and you may judge by the result. GOD has His reasons for removing this sense of resistance, though you really continue to resist. It is His will that you should not attribute the victory to your own exertions, and grow vain and self-complacent on the strength of it. Is it not well, that the honour should be given where it is due, and that GOD should place you in happy inability to rob Him of it?

"But I believe I do yield my consent!" On what grounds? Because the temptation lasts a long time? That is no valid reason; it only proves that the struggle is long. Or is it because the ideas which are intruded into your mind cause it a sense of pleasure? There is an involuntary delectation, an impression on the senses, which is the natural effect of certain temptations. This may be caused by a heated imagination, or by Satan himself. But, in themselves, such feelings have nothing in common with consent. Do not decide for yourself in this matter; in your present state of agitation you are unfit to pass judgment on yourself. Beware of even thinking of temptation, when once it has passed away, and do not attempt to trace its progress from the beginning. This is very dangerous, and all masters of the spiritual life forbid it. Refer the matter to your confessor; and when he shall have given a general decision and confirmed it repeatedly, trust to it without demur.

The Christian's arms against Satan are watchfulness and prayer. "Watch and pray, that ye enter not into temptation." It is impossible that the soul of man should escape temptation. Therefore He said not, "Watch and pray, that ye be not tempted," but, "that ye enter not into temptation;" *i.e.*, that ye fall not under temptation.

We must needs watch against an adversary who is both subtle and violent, and who, "as a roaring lion walketh about, seeking whom he may devour." Watchfulness is necessary for all men, how holy soever they be. Any one who is not on his guard, is, for that very reason, in danger from the devil; the danger is greater for a righteous man who presumes on his strength, than for a sinner who dreads the result of his weakness. Remember our LORD'S words: "What I say unto you I say unto all, Watch!"

Watchfulness consists, in the first place, in shunning occasions of temptation. We must never wilfully expose ourselves under any pretext. In the second place, it consists in a humble distrust of ourselves. "I was in misery," [I humbled myself: *Vulgate:*] "and He helped me." He cannot utterly fall who is lowly in his own eyes and leans only on the LORD; he who trusts in himself cannot but be overcome. Victory itself is fatal to him.

Do not confound (as is often the case) mistrust

of self with faint-heartedness. The faint-hearted looks no further than himself, and, comparing his danger with his weakness, turns to fly when he ought to fight. The truly humble Christian looks at once on his own weakness and the might of GOD. When bidden to the strife he fears nothing; on the contrary, the more he feels his own inability to resist, the more he trusts that Almighty strength will sustain him. "When I am weak then am I strong. I can do all things through CHRIST Which strengtheneth me."

Watchfulness consists moreover in unshaken faithfulness. Hold fast to the practice of contemplative prayer and interior mortification; follow out minutely all the guidance GOD may have given you. Observe every particular of the rule which you have laid down for yourself, or which has been prescribed for you. Allow yourself in no wilful breach of duty, and the devil will be powerless against you; all his assaults will turn to his own confusion.

Take great care never to be agitated by the onset of temptation; do not let your mind dwell on what is passing within you; do not argue with the devil. You will only be entangled in your own thoughts, and he will wrap his nets about you. Hide beneath the wings of GOD, and let the cloud pass over you. Disquiet and brooding thoughts only increase and prolong the storm, and draw it more fiercely down upon your head. When it has spent itself, go quietly on your way, without searching to discover whether you took pleasure in the temptation, or yielded consent to it.

To watchfulness our LORD bids us add prayer, and both must be constantly persevered in; for He taught that "Men ought always to pray and not to faint." This continual prayer is, as has been said elsewhere, the direction of the heart towards God: the hidden invocation of His help. How can the devil injure a soul thus disposed, and thus covered by the buckler of prayer?

But beside the general attitude of prayer, from which the soul should never cease, it is a good practice, when temptation arises, to take refuge, if possible, in your closet, or in the presence of the Blessed Sacrament; or, if that be impracticable, have recourse to ejaculatory prayers, which are so many arrows wherewith to wound the foe. And let these prayers be quickened by confidence; let them be calm and submissive. Do not ask impatiently for the withdrawal of the temptation. Such petitions often arise from self-love. You are cast down at being subjected to such horrible thoughts, and you seek freedom from that humiliation. But humiliation is one of the best effects of temptation, and therefore God permits it. Yield yourself wholly to God, and suffer temptation so long as shall be His good pleasure. He only knows what good is wrought by temptations; He has set a fixed time for their removal; it will take place the moment you have profited by them as fully as it is God's will you should.

Temptations are the counterpoise of graces received; and our graces are always the exact measure of our temptations. We delight in graces which raise us up; and we fear temptations which abase us. But such abasement is the effect of grace, yea, of greater grace than that we previously enjoyed, for it shields us against those dangers to which other graces expose us.

However horrible and humiliating may be your temptations, never hide them from your director;

but open your heart to him, and let him know all you feel. GOD blesses such a disclosure, which is in itself a great act of humility. He always connects many graces with it, and inspires your director to strengthen and encourage you as He sees best. But the devil strives by all means to silence those he tempts; he is confident of success, if only he can persuade them to keep obstinate silence.

By means of your appointed guide you will receive peace, light, and strength. His decisions will tranquillize, his counsels wiil enlighten, his exhortations will quicken. But then, after having fully explained yourself, rely wholly on his decisions; do not allow yourself to judge otherwise than he has judged, even in thought. Do not say: "I did not rightly explain the true state of things;" or, "he did not understand me." It would make matters interminable, and you would never be persuaded that he is in the right. Acquiesce and submit; and moreover be most sedulous in using all such means as he directs, whether for prevention or abatement of temptation, or for gaining victory over it.

SEVENTEENTH MAXIM.

Beware of self-love, the rival of the love of God.

"*I will go forth in the strength of the Lord God, and will make mention of Thy righteousness only.*"

XVII.

OF SELF-LOVE.

NOTHING better marks the character of self-love, or should make it more hateful to us, than this title: Rival of the love of GOD. "Our loves form our manners," says S. Augustine. We can bestow our whole love on but one only of two objects: GOD or self. To set GOD above all things, and refer all to Him, is to be actuated by charity: divine love, rendering us good and pleasing in His sight, imparting to our actions a value above their desert, and perfecting us in proportion to its purity and simplicity. To refer all things to self, is to be filled with self-love; a love vicious and inordinate, utterly displeasing to GOD, vitiating actions otherwise most holy, and rendering us more and more wicked in proportion to the sway it exercises in our hearts.

These two loves are entirely contrary to one another; not only rivals but enemies, disputing the possession of the same heart. No compact can exist between them. They hate, attack, and persecute each other to the death. The perfect extinction of self-love, either in this world or the next, opens heaven for us, and ensures our blessedness. The extinction of the love of God, when we pass out of this life, sinks us into hell, and constitutes our eternal misery.

So soon as a Christian really gives himself to God and to His service, divine love takes possession of his heart, sets up its throne within it, and forthwith proceeds to drive out self-love. Then self-love endeavours to maintain itself intact; if driven from one quarter it takes refuge in another; and so retreats from hold to hold, till it hides in the inmost recesses of the soul. This is its last refuge, and it is very difficult to tear it thence. There is no device by which it does not endeavour to injure and weaken the enemy, and to lessen, if it cannot prevent, its victory. It is always dangerous, even after defeat; and often, when we think it crushed to the earth, it arises more formidable than ever.

Such is the enemy, which we have to fight with the aid of grace. An enemy born with us, and in some sort a part of our very selves. Age, passions, habits, thoughts, good qualities, and sometimes even virtues, contribute to strengthen its hold upon us. We so confuse it with ourselves that it seems impossible to disentangle it, and the idea of destroying it involves apparent danger to our very existence.

How powerless must we be against an enemy so well-beloved, and holding so powerful a position? The saddest thing is, that it blinds us, and deprives us of all power of perceiving it. We can only discern it by the light of grace, which unveils its devices, opens our eyes to its impending strokes, teaches us to ward them off, and strengthens us to fight against it. If we pay no heed to this light, or lose it by our own fault, we are left wholly defenceless, unable not only to conquer, but even to resist; unable to see our enemy, and incredulous of his being such. Our blindness, on the contrary, is so gross, that it leads us to take him for a friend and confidant most dear and hearty.

This wretched blindness is the common disease of Christians, and even of the more devout. It is the more baneful because unperceived and unsuspected, and thus there is exceeding difficulty in convincing the mind of its existence and presence. We are mostly more or less in the condition of the Pharisees, who, with regard to our LORD, were blinded by arrogant self-love, and yet fancied themselves clear-sighted. He said to them: "Ye say, we see, therefore your sin remaineth;" and by your wilfulness ye fill up the measure of that iniquity which ye should rather abhor.

We may assume as a fact, without fear of mistake, that we are blind on many points concerning our perfection, and, perhaps, salvation. We should continually pray that GOD would enlighten us, either directly by His Spirit, or indirectly by the advice of friends or the censure of enemies. In whatever way light may come, it is a blessing sent by GOD. We ought to welcome and receive it gratefully, encourage others to offer it, and neglect nothing that may lead us to profit by it. This is a tone of mind most earnestly to be prayed for, and one to which most of our natural tendencies are directly opposed. We must be on our guard (I will not say against flattery; I assume that directors and spiritual friends are incapable of offering that for our acceptance—

but even) against acts and words of respect and consideration; especially if our rank, or age, or temperament seem to exact them. We ought to take it for granted that our faults are passed over, or made light of, by the discretion or kind-heartedness of those with whom we have to do; that we are praised, not for what we are, but for what we might be. When we are blamed, let our own hearts add to what is mentioned as blameworthy. When we are praised, let us mentally deprecate our right to the praise bestowed on us. Thus we may keep watch against ourselves and our bosom enemy, self-love.

We will now look more closely into the various devices used by self-love for the corruption of true piety. Its chief aim is to appropriate the work of grace, and rob GOD of the glory of good actions, or claim a share in such glory; thus robbing us of all merit, for that is based wholly on humility. So S. Philip Neri said to the LORD: "Beware of me, as of a great robber." Self-love is jealous of the property of GOD, and endeavours to rob Him of it. This property is the glory which belongs to GOD alone, and which He cannot give to another. He allows us to make use of His blessings, but all glory must be rendered back to Him. This is exactly what self-love desires to appropriate, prompting us to glory in ourselves, against the express precept of the Apostle: "He that glorieth, let him glory in the LORD."

But when it would enrich us at the expense of GOD, self-love makes us poor indeed. For there is no merit, nor reward, nor blessing, except for those who, owning their spiritual poverty, attributing nothing to and appropriating nothing to themselves, render thanks to God for all the good that is in them, and refer all to Him from Whom all proceeds. God is jealous, and the chief effect of His jealousy is that, as every good gift proceeds from Him, so it is His will that man should render homage for it, and acknowledge that he holds all from the hand of God. A pauper, admitted by God to share His riches, must never forget his intrinsic poverty and the free bounty of his Benefactor. If he becomes puffed up and self-complacent, he deserves to lose all.

Self-love is mercenary ; in the service of God it looks to its own interests, without rising to higher considerations. A soul tainted with this poison, desires holiness as an embellishing ornament and distinguishing perfection. It desires to be pure, but only in order to contemplate its own purity ; it fears sin, less as an offence against God than as a spot on the brilliancy of its own beauty. It is more astonished than abashed by its faults, scarcely conceiving how it was possible for it to fall ; its repentance savours more of vexation than of regret ; and what it believes to be an act of contrition and love of God, is merely an act of inordinate self-love.

Self-love is greedy of consolations ; it seeks them from God and from men ; enjoys them with clinging eagerness, regrets them bitterly when removed ; and, if the privation lasts too long for its fancy, it relaxes its fidelity, complains and murmurs and threatens to turn back from all good living, as if God were worthy of being served only for His gifts. And all this time it is artful enough to persuade us that we are generous, disinterested, and actuated by the purest love of God.

Self-love is vain and presumptuous in time of abundance and spiritual prosperity; at such times it leads us not to calculate our real strength, but imagines itself capable of anything: it broods over the promises and declarations which it offers to GOD; and though they be but vain unfruitful words, it leads us to regard them as solid proofs of our own devotedness. But in dearth and adversity it is cast down, despondent, and incapable of the slightest effort.

It loves a sort of holiness that is quiet, comfortable, and easy-going, involving no suffering for mind or body, and few or no obstacles to be overcome; such holiness as may be acquired quickly and cheaply, is to be had for the wishing, and (to use an expression of S. Francis de Sales) may be slipped on like a dress. That is to say, self-love evokes an empty phantom of holiness, wishing to be holy without taking any steps to become so. Therefore it is soft, indolent, lazy, full of unfruitful desires, impatient, repelled by the slightest difficulties, weary and exhausted as soon as the first step has been taken. No mention must be made of steep ascents; self-love requires a road either level or of easy acclivity. So long as nothing unpleasant occurs, it advances readily; but if called on to contradict a favourite inclination, overcome a repugnance, or meet a temptation, it straightway loses courage, stops short or turns back.

Self-love does not affect such virtue as is humble, obscure, unobserved of men: still less, despised, spoken against, and persecuted. Good deeds done in secret, with no sounding of trumpets, are not to its taste; it loves to show itself in full daylight; it seeks display, consideration, esteem and applause, which it secures artfully, invites deprecatingly, and receives hypocritically. In these things it delights, while it pretends to reject them; if the world withholds them, it supplies itself with them in secret.

It hates simplicity and common every-day life; it affects singularity, and defines holiness as consisting, not in the perfect performance of ordinary actions, but in a course of extraordinary conduct. Nothing in its habits is regular, sustained, or constant; all is fanciful, capricious, and changeful.

It is always wishing to make sure that it has done well, that its conduct is approved by God, and still more by the director; hence arise ever repeated introspections, with uneasy and scrupulous testings of motives and intentions; and an unceasing exacting of testimonials, from conscience, from God in prayer, and from the director in the confessional or elsewhere. All this, so it asserts, is done in order to gain firmness, support, and encouragement. This is a vain pretext. It is with the purpose of finding occasion for self-gratulation, food for vanity, or at least an assurance of progress made, and the comfort of some light on the weary darkness of a way which provides no visible support.

Self-love is ever occupied in comparisons: exulting in superiority, or vexed and annoyed if forced to yield to others. It blames all conduct but its own: its own way of prayer must be the best; or else it envies souls which it supposes to be more advanced and more favoured of God. It notes the faults of others, criticises actions, judges and condemns motives, and ever whispers to itself: "I would not have acted thus; I would not have spoken thus, under the same circumstances." Its most terrible characteristic is the spiritual jealousy, which gnaws and tortures it. Persons thus affected think that their director never pays them sufficient attention; they are neglected, while all care is lavished upon others. When others were spoken to, when written to, when and how often visited—all this they pry into and complain of; and if these complaints do not receive all the regard supposed to be their due, which is a thing impossible, then the anger of the aggrieved passes all bounds. The miserable effects of this jealousy extend to GOD Himself; He is sometimes, forsooth, accused of showing more favour to those than to these: who set forth to Him how innocent have been their lives, how excellent their exercises and austerities; and, like the prodigal's elder brother, they reproach the Father with the welcome given to those who have not served Him as they have done.

Self-love accustoms the soul to claim as its own those gifts and graces with which GOD endows it. Therefore it is very impatient of GOD'S seeming withdrawal of them; clings to them passionately, and is perfectly miserable when apparently deprived of them. Not that GOD does actually remove His gifts, for He always leaves the roots of virtue in the soul; but He acts in such wise that it no longer perceives their presence, in order that it may cease to look on them as its own; and to this end He allows temptations contrary to these virtues; feelings of distaste and repugnance with regard to them; upheavings of passion in the lower nature, to which the soul never really consents, although it seems to itself to do so; and He withdraws all power of self-appreciation, even to the perception of virtuous acts performed.

Lastly, God is the true centre of the soul; self-love robs Him of this right, and fixes the centre in the soul itself. This is what may be called appropriation, a deep-seated, radical vice, which has become so much a part of man's nature, that he has much ado to perceive it, understand its mischievous character, and consent to be delivered from it by God. However advanced a soul may be, it would never give up this secret reference to self, which leads it to consider both its perfection and its blessedness from a selfish point of view, not subordinate to the glory and will of God: this renunciation would never be made, unless God exerted the constraining and absolute control over its free-will, which the soul has already surrendered into His hands. That is self-love's last stronghold, and its last and deepest working place, with reference to which S. Francis de Sales said: "It would be well if this vice died in us a quarter of an hour before we die ourselves."

Self-love is the one source of all illusions in the spiritual life. By its means the devil exercises sleights, leads souls astray, drags them sometimes to hell by the very road that seems to lead to heaven. We long eagerly for spiritual delights: the devil gives false pleasures, which feed vanity and sensuousness; we wish ardently for extraordinary favours: the devil transforms himself into an angel of light, and counterfeits the Divine operations. We question God curiously on our own state and that of others, and on secret or future events: the devil causes us to hear an inward voice, which we mistake for an answer from heaven. Then we fancy ourselves the recipients of peculiar light, and grow wilful, obstinate, and deaf to good advice; we shake off the yoke of authority, and, under the deceitful guise of sanctity, conceal the pride of Lucifer.

I have only set forth the perversions and disorders introduced by self-love into devotion. What if I were to speak of those which creep, by its assistance, into the exercise of the most sacred offices, such as the preaching of God's word and the direction of souls? I do not allude to those ministers who regard a pious way of life as a means of acquiring reputation or riches, and assume the duties of preaching the gospel and spiritual guidance through interested motives. Such motives are so gross, and so plainly reprobated in Holy Scripture, that no one can cheat himself respecting their sinfulness. But who can enumerate the miserable littlenesses and rivalries which beset some preachers and confessors, who are otherwise pious and estimable men? We will not dwell on a subject which can only be a scandal and a stumbling-block. But I may say, that no man can examine himself too strictly on this point, nor be too careful in investigating—not whether in the discharge of duty he sometimes feels natural weaknesses; none, alas! are free from them: but—whether, by reason of these infirmities, he humbles himself before God, and diligently strives to resist and overcome them.

I shall not enter upon the discussion of the specious reasonings with which self-love skilfully conceals itself. It is too wary to appear in its true colours; it would then manifestly be too despicable, too odious. One would blush to give ear to it. It assumes the fairest colourings, and the most seductive guise. Its motive is always zeal for GOD's glory; its aim is the perfection of one's own soul, or the spiritual welfare of others. Its true purpose lies hidden in the depths of the heart; it professes other objects which are good and holy, adroitly intermingles them with its views, and deceives by means of the admixture.

The remedy for so great an evil in the practice of devotion, is to allow ourselves to depend on nothing that we feel or even see, but to rise higher, and cling to GOD alone, and His good pleasure. We are always safe while we consider piety, not as it concerns self, but wholly as it concerns GOD. Therefore, the way of bare faith, in which we walk, as it were, blindly, without evidence or assurance, shelters us from all illusion. Therefore, too, GOD so carefully hides His work from us, and forbids us to pry into it. Self-love wishes to take part in everything, to see all, in order everywhere to find material to feed on: and therefore GOD conceals everything from it.

Then let us cease from uneasy consideration of self, and never look at ourselves from motives of curiosity, complacency, or selfishness. We should forget ourselves, and rest wholly in GOD, putting in practice the exhortation given by our LORD to S. Katharine of Sienna: "My daughter, think of Me, and I will think of thee." This short but pregnant expression comprises all perfection; and shows that GOD is busied with our true interests in proportion as we are busied with His. All faults committed in the inner life, all hindrances and obstacles encountered, all uneasiness and misery, arise only from this reason, that we look at and think of self, instead of thinking of GOD, and trusting His goodness, wisdom, and love for all things. I am aware that perfect forgetfulness of self is attained only by slow degrees; but it must be our continual intention, and we must practise ourselves in acts of that virtue at every opportunity; and such opportunities are of constant recurrence, because we are so near to ourselves. "Wherever you find yourself," said the author of the Imitation, "there leave yourself." The practical application of this precept is unlimited: it is utterly grievous to self-love, and therefore infinitely profitable to the soul. It embraces everything, and excepts nothing: "*Wherever* you find yourself." Measure your progress by your fidelity in following this rule; or rather, if you possibly can, be faithful to it without thinking that you are so.

"Love to be unknown and to be made of no account." This is another counsel given by the same author. Self-love intensely dreads obscurity, it is tenacious of being seen, known, and esteemed. Do not allege duty to God and to men. Seek to be hidden. God will be able to find and use you when needful for His glory and the salvation of souls. But as far as you are yourself free to choose, always avoid such positions as are likely to involve publicity and notice, and then publicity will do you no harm when, in spite of yourself, you are exposed to it. When you are no longer likely to be injured by temptations to vanity, and when reputation for holiness will be no snare for you, then God will make use of you, and produce you before the world.

Be glad that God Himself should treat you as unknown and of no account. Love to see His consolations and favours bestowed on others, while hardness and loneliness are your portion. After all, what are you? What do you deserve? And what should you desire, but that GOD should deal justly with you in this world by treating you as a sinner and a thing of nought?

In the last place, be sure that "you will advance only in proportion as you do violence to self." Allow no quarter, no forbearance to self-love; you must pursue that criminal to the death, and ceaselessly ask his destruction at the hands of GOD. "Burn, cut off on earth," as S. Augustine said, "if only Thou grant me mercy in eternity." This seems barbarous and horrible to nature, but in practice it is sweeter than men suppose: here the soul finds peace and happiness. The more self-love is brought under control, the greater is our freedom, independence and serenity.

Then let us boldly go out to battle against this foe to peace and holiness. Let us carry our attacks to the greatest possible extent, praying that GOD Himself will deal the final blow; we may hasten the end, but complete victory lies in GOD's hands alone.

EIGHTEENTH MAXIM.

Stay quietly at home; regulate your day, and waste no time.

"*Study to be quiet, and to do your own business.*"

XVIII.

OF A RETIRED LIFE.

LOVE of retirement and solitude disposes the soul peculiarly for the practice of an interior life. "I will bring her into the wilderness, and speak comfortably unto her." When a man is alone with his own soul, and undisturbed by the excitement of external things, unless he is beset by violent passion, his reflections naturally turn first to himself and then lead him back to GOD.

I do not mean that persons living in the world should lead a life of retirement, such as is practised in convents and hermitages. Living at home, going out merely as duty requires, is living in retirement. Having no dealings with the world, but such as are required by necessity or charity, is living in solitude. He who loves to be alone with GOD, and, amid the turmoil of business, longs for the time when he may hold free converse with Him, has already, or soon will have, entered upon the interior life.

Take advantage then of all the leisure your affairs allow, reserve some part of every day to be spent in the consideration of eternal things. These are most valuable moments, which, if used aright, will enable you to sanctify the rest of the day.

Another holy practice, which draws down many graces, is that of yearly setting apart one week as a time of retreat, spent in undisturbed meditation on the truths pertaining to salvation, and in serious examination of the state of the soul; setting it in order, and making thorough and earnest preparation for the future. This practice was formerly common, but has fallen into disuse; much of the interior spirit has departed with it.

Silence is one of the first fruits of a retired life; it conduces greatly to collectedness and prayer, and its practice cannot be too strongly urged. The interior spirit reigns, or soon will reign, in every community where silence is stedfastly observed. Fidelity to that rule is the safeguard of all others. Laxity and disorder gradually creep into convents where it is disregarded.

In the world it is not easy to fix certain hours for silence, because occasions for speaking occur, when least expected. But the spirit of silence is kept, if we only speak as is opportune and necessary; if, in company, without affecting ill-placed taciturnity, we listen rather than talk; and if, when we talk, we keep vivacity in due bounds, and use that reticence which is inspired by the Spirit of GOD. This reticence is one of the marks by which our LORD was to be known. "He shall not cry, nor lift up, nor cause His voice to be heard in the street;" and, among pious persons, those who cultivate the inner life are readily distinguishable by this sign. Their conversation is not therefore less natural; it is only more pleasant and interesting; and, though tempered by a certain reserve, it is neither dull, cold, nor constrained.

When the soul is in its first religious fervour, it needs no exhortation to retirement and silence; it is naturally inclined to seek them. The loss of spiritual delights is then too much dreaded, the secret brooding over them is too sweet, to allow any wish for distraction from without. Intercourse with worldly persons is oppressive; it seems merely a painful void, and is carefully shunned, and perhaps too much so to meet the demands of our position, and those of Christian charity.

But a fault then imminent is that of bestowing indiscreet confidence on persons with whom we are intimate, of pouring out our feelings too freely, and telling them of our own happiness in the hope of bringing them to God. We feel unable to contain the grace that fills us, and find comfort in sharing our secret with others. But we should do better in keeping it to ourselves, and mentioning it only to our confessor. The inner workings of grace are not to be divulged; they must be kept hidden, and we are not to pretend to the apostolate, while we are as yet but weak neophytes.

But when spiritual spring-time is past, and dryness has succeeded to refreshment, there is reason to fear lest we give up our retired life and seek intercourse with created things. This natural inclination must be resisted as a most dangerous temptation, which exposes the rising structure of our perfection to imminent ruin. Though we then no longer feel the presence of God, He yet is present with us more deeply and ineffably, and in a manner which we can easily apprehend, if we be extremely careful to retain it. All voluntary distraction of mind aims a blow at this real, but unperceived recollectedness; it leaves impressions on the imagination which are revived during prayer; and the more easily, because in a state of dryness the soul is empty of ideas and feelings. Prayer thus becomes a continual distraction, which is sinful (at least in so far as we have brought it on ourselves); and besides, as we already find contemplative prayer difficult, receiving, as it seems to us, no help from God, it is soon given up. With it we give up the inner life.

It is not enough to stay at home, quiet and silent, we must also arrange our time, and so distribute the occupations of the day, that every duty shall have its appointed time, and every hour its duty. We shall thus avoid listlessness, wearied want of employment, and the consequent temptations.

The chief point is to fix the hours for rising and going to bed, for on that the rest depends. Then we must distribute our devotional exercises, —mental prayer, church services, reading, vocal prayer, and other pious practices—in such wise that some may be given to the morning and some to the evening, and no long period may elapse without religious acts. The time which remains at our disposal should be devoted to work, and to the requirements of our condition in life.

However, as God desires that we should be slaves only to His love and His will, which is above all other rule, and many accidents may derange the regulation of our day, we must bend to the disposal of His Providence, and not reproach ourselves with omissions which it was out of our power to avoid. We are faithful, if we are as faithful as we are able to be. Exactness with regard to GOD, lies less in the fulfilling of the letter than in the disposition of the will. To break the rules of charity, propriety, and courtesy, in order to observe our rule of time, would be a want of fidelity to GOD. True piety is in no wise opposed to the fulfilment of the duties of society; it sanctifies our relations with our neighbour, even when they seem most trifling, and are only dependent on custom and politeness; it does not require us to renounce them, nor does it even allow us to neglect them.

Therefore, in the first place, we must so arrange our rule that we may be able to observe it habitually; not overburdening it with practices, nor multiplying them excessively; this fetters the spirit and enslaves the soul; we must consider our health, position, occupations, and the persons on whom we depend, such as a mother or husband; to which persons we owe the greatest deference. Next, when interrupted, whether by unforeseen business, letters, or visits to be paid or received, we must not scruple to give up the devotional exercise assigned to the time thus engrossed, but resume it at some other period, if possible; we must not make ourselves odious or ridiculous by mistimed exactitude; nor show by our air and bearing that we are disturbed, and had other things to do; but gracefully lend ourselves not only to friends, but to troublesome and importunate persons. GOD permits these little crosses for the breaking of our will, and in order to give us free and pliable devotion, like that of S. Francis de Sales; and to lead us to the practice of many virtues, which have no place but under such circumstances.

In the last place, for the prevention of all scruples, we must distinctly and carefully decide as to what does and what does not depend upon ourselves; what we are at liberty to do, and what would annoy those whom we are bound to consider. We must distinguish such practices as maintain us in a state of holy freedom, without trenching on the bounds of true fidelity, from such as breathe the spirit of bondage and involve constraint, hair-splitting, and exaggerated stiffness. If we are honest with ourselves and with GOD, we can always decide easily whether or no we are to blame for any non-observance of our rule.

Such regulations can of course only be made by those whose time is chiefly at their disposal. But other persons, if earnestly desirous to advance in holy living, will make use of all spare moments, and carefully husband the time they may call their own, in order to employ it in prayer and holy reading. They must not complain of the hardship of their position; it is ordered by Providence, and will not hinder their advance, if they are drawn towards an interior life. GOD Himself will more than make up to them for the want of ordinary means, and perhaps their busy hampered condition will tend more to their sanctification than a state of perfect leisure and independence. There are no obstacles for those who are determined to love GOD.

Many reasons should induce this regulation of time, when practicable. First, the absolute and universal duty of sanctifying our actions. Now we already begin to sanctify them, if we order them by a fixed rule reasonably supposed to be according to GOD's will, and if we then perform each at its own hour, as if at the very summons of GOD.

Next, when exercises of piety are ordered by rule, they are less easily forgotten and sooner become habitual. The very hour reminds us of our duty, and also frequently gives occasion for some act of self-denial in laying aside what we are about, in order to obey our LORD'S will.

Then, we avoid idleness, which is a great temptation for those whose time is at their own disposal. We are all naturally inclined to repose and laziness. But there is no fear of indolence for those whose time is all marked out; imagination is not on the stretch as to what shall be done or left undone; every hour has its appointed task, and the different occupations which continually succeed each other do not allow the spirits to flag. Thus we are delivered from ennui, the terrible scourge of an unoccupied life.

And if protected from indolence and ennui, how many temptations are shut out from the soul! How many occasions of sin are shunned!

What I have now said refers to all Christians in general, according to their various circumstances. But as to those who lead an interior life, they are more inclined to regulate their time than others, and they observe their regulations more faithfully. The Spirit of GOD, in Whom they live and by Whom they are led, suffers them no indefinite course of life, and demands a strict account of all their time. But their rule is not changeless; it must alter according to the various stages through which they pass. Practices which are useful at first, are not afterwards suitable. The Spirit of GOD sometimes forbids what at other times He commands. Exercises proper to retirement should occupy the first years. Afterwards GOD leaves them more at liberty to mix in external matters for the benefit of others. At one time, those practices are necessary which lead to introversion ; at another they ought to do such things as draw them out of themselves and render self-forgetfulness obligatory. In times of peculiar and violent temptation, a wise director will allow amusements and innocent diversions, which are then necessary, and which he may have rightly forbidden in other circumstances. I say no more on this point, because I am not writing for advanced souls, but for beginners.

NINETEENTH MAXIM.

Let charity and piety begin at home.

"*He hath showed thee, O man, what is good; and what doth the Lord require of thee, but to do justly, and to love mercy, and to walk humbly with thy God?*"

XIX.

OF DISCRETION.

NEGLECT of business and domestic duties, under a pretext of piety, is common enough. Devotees, especially of the female sex, often fall into this error, and so give scandal even to sensible and really religious persons. Yet devotion is not herein to blame, but rather that self-will which is followed instead of the Spirit of GOD.

Many have no sooner undertaken the practice of piety, than they begin to neglect their homes, their children, and their servants; they spend the day in going to church, run after popular preachers, attend every religious meeting and special festival, and undertake all manner of good works. They are to be found everywhere excepting at home, but they leave that as early, and return to it as late, as possible.

Meanwhile all is disorder in the household;

every one does as he pleases while the mistress is away; children are left to the careless hands of those who themselves need watching, or are dragged about, especially if girls, from service to service; they are wearied out and disgusted, and soon learn to dislike religion. The husband justly complains. but his words are unheeded, and are secretly attributed to a want of religion.

And thus it is also with many men, who are active, bustling, busy-bodies; meddling in everything under pretence of serving God; fancying that the whole Church depends on them, while they scarcely ever give a thought to themselves. Many priests are not irreproachable in this respect. They have zeal, but not according to knowledge. They yield unreservedly to natural activity.; and, because their ministry really embraces many objects, they intrude beyond their province, and imagine that everything is in their hands. They will recommend husbands, or suggest vocations for young women, arrange money matters between disputing parties, and act as registry-offices for servants out of place. They must manage all good works, or success is not to be expected. They pry into family secrets, even in the confessional. They govern the households of their penitents, regulate their expenses, manage their estates, attend to their lawsuits, and draw up their wills. They are for ever, and everywhere, coming and going. The day is not long enough for all they have to do; they must needs borrow from the night, and have scarcely time to say their own office.

I do not mean to criticise; nothing is further from my inclination and the intention of this book. But how can I do otherwise than lament over an evil such as this, which is so harmful to religion? I do not blame the intention, I believe it to be right and pure; nor the object, which is good, because it concerns the worship of GOD and the welfare of men. But who can love to see the order of duty reversed, and works of supererogation taking precedence of obligatory duties? Who can excuse the mistaken piety which looks merely to externals, and counts the inner spirit as nothing, but neglects GOD's primary laws?

The spirit of the inner life follows another course, and inspires very opposite ideas. It teaches all who yield to its guidance, that their primary duty is the sanctification of their own souls, and that the holiness of a Christian consists chiefly in the fulfilment of the duties of his station. These are indispensable: the very end of devotion is the obtaining of such graces as are necessary for their fulfilment. It can therefore never be a reason for neglecting them; on the contrary, true piety allows that time only for prayer which can lawfully be spared from imperative duties; and bids us in all religious exercises, not of strict obligation, to accommodate ourselves to the wishes and weakness of those whom we are bound to consider, and, for peace' sake, to sacrifice our own tastes, be they never so pious.

The spirit of true religion teaches ministers of the Gospel, that the care of souls ought to be limited to things spiritual, and it only allows interference in temporal matters when charity requires it of them, and then with much reserve and circumspection, both lest they should injure themselves, and lest they should lessen in the minds of others the reverence due to their office.

These things would be taught by the spirit of the inner life, if men sought its guidance with a pure heart. Thus it taught Ambrose, Augustine, Chrysostom, Borromeo, Francis de Sales, and every other Saint and Doctor of the Church.

heaven. Then we fancy ourselves th of peculiar light, and grow wilful, ob deaf to good advice; we shake off authority, and, under the deceitful gu tity, conceal the pride of Lucifer.

I have only set forth the perve disorders introduced by self-love int What if I were to speak of those whic its assistance, into the exercise of sacred offices, such as the preaching word and the direction of souls? I do to those ministers who regard a pious as a means of acquiring reputation or assume the duties of preaching the spiritual guidance through intereste Such motives are so gross, and so pla bated in Holy Scripture, that no one himself respecting their sinfulness. Bu enumerate the miserable littlenesses an which beset some preachers and confesso otherwise pious and estimable men? W dwell on a subject which can only be a sc a stumbling-block. But I may say, tha can examine himself too strictly on th nor be too careful in investigating—no in the discharge of duty he sometimes fee weaknesses; none, alas! are free from the whether, by reason of these infirmities, he himself before GOD, and diligently s resist and overcome them.

I shall not enter upon the discussi specious reasonings with which self- fully conceals itself. It is too wary to its true colours; it would then manifes despicable, too odious. One would blus ear to it. It assumes the fairest colouring

most seductive guise. Its
for God's glory; its aim is
own soul, or the spiritual
true purpose lies hidden
heart; it professes other
and holy, adroitly inter
views, and deceives by m

The remedy for so gr
of devotion, is to allow
nothing that we feel
higher, and cling to G
pleasure. We are alway
piety, not as it
concerns God. Therefore
in which we walk, as it
evidence or assurance
Therefore, too, God
from us, and forsakes us
wishes to take part
order everywhere
therefore God

Then let us
self, and never
curiosity
forget
in practise
S. Katharine of
Me, and I will
pregnant
shown that God
in proportion
faults
and
misery
at and
and waiting

TWENTIETH MAXIM.

Be cordial and kind, gentle and lowly; tender to your neighbours, and hard upon yourself.

"*Above all these things put on charity, which is the bond of perfectness.*"

XX.

OF INTERCOURSE WITH OTHERS.

VIRTUE is essentially lovely. Where it is not so, it is imperfect; and its imperfection is due to self-love and self-esteem. When humility has dried up these two sources of all our shortcomings and evil habits, then virtue shows herself in full loveliness, and all must do her homage, even though unavowed. For virtue obliges us to transfer to others the feelings we have entertained for self; so that the sentiment which, when directed towards ourselves, was unrighteous self-love, is transformed into righteous charity when bestowed on others. It leads us to do as we would be done by; to think, and speak, and endure with regard to them, as we would have them do with regard to us. Certainly no one could refuse the tribute of love to virtue like this; and, if all men were virtuous, love would be universally reciprocal.

Thus, then, true piety inspires all loveliness, and its first sign is gentleness. A true servant of GOD is austere towards himself only, and that according to discretion. But towards others he is kind, easy, and yielding, so far as his conscience will allow. If sometimes forced to be severe, charity is the rule of such severity. When we intend to live religiously in the world, we mistake the line we ought to take, if we break off all social relations, and devote ourselves wholly to pious exercises. Because we belong to GOD, is it any reason that we should have no friends, if our friendships are not in themselves of a reprehensible character? Why deprive ourselves of the pleasure of society? Why should courteous visits be a weariness to us? Why not even put up with such as are useless or tiresome? What can the world think of devotees who shut themselves up at home, deny themselves to every visitor, and show a repulsive or embarrassed face to all who accost them? By thus withdrawing from all social intercourse, we make piety odious, and give the impression that its practice is impossible; we deprive ourselves of many opportunities of exercising virtue; we contract evil habits, and a turn of mind alien to true religion.

Undoubtedly it is well to fix hours for our religious duties, and, as far as possible, to discharge them faithfully; but then they ought not to be so numerous as to leave us no time to bestow on our fellow-creatures. Besides, charity skilfully accommodates itself to circumstances, and at fitting times gives up devout exercises to the courtesy due towards others.

Moreover, true piety shows much gentleness in the exercise of authority over children, servants, or dependents; it is not rigid, imperious, and exacting; not severe in rebuke; it does not take notice of every trifling offence; it is ready to forgive; threats are not always on its lips, nor chastisement in its hand. It especially avoids outbursts of impatience and anger, hard words, reproaches, and all that mortifies and offends without helping to correct. It seeks after good, but not harshly, and does not expect perfection to be attained in a moment. It waits patiently, and returns again and again to the same point; it consoles, encourages, has a good word for good-will, and praises slight efforts in order to induce greater.

But the especial point which the practice of piety corrects in our social character is querulousness. We all understand the term, though it may perhaps be impossible to define it. It is laid to the charge of devout persons more than of other men; mistaken devoutness often gives occasion for its display. The cross humour to which I allude does not spring from a root of wickedness; it is not the failing of the bad and crafty, but on the contrary of the frank and straightforward. But it causes many misdoings of which one is heartily ashamed when the fit has passed, and it is insupportable in society. Politeness teaches us to check it in the presence of strangers and persons whom we respect; but it is amply indulged before intimate friends and at home. And those who yield to it are the first to suffer from its effects.

Nothing is more difficult to extirpate than this cross temper, because it is not excited by any particular reason nor by any recognized moral cause, and it depends in great measure upon physical causes; besides, it forestals preparation, and its fits come on when least expected. What hold can the will effect on such disease when middle life has been attained? I know but one remedy: the practice of the presence of God and of contemplative prayer. The presence of God awakens attention to the first stirrings of cross humour, and checks them; prayer gradually fixes the mind in a state of evenness, keeps imagination in bounds, lessens sensitiveness, and puts low spirits to flight; and these, I think, are the chief springs of ill humour. Indeed, it is plainly to be seen that persons who lead a life of prayer are not subject to this disease; and so much cannot be said of others.

The gentleness imparted by virtue, differs from that which is merely natural. Those who are gentle by nature are often weak, soft, indifferent, apathetic, and excessively indulgent. But those whom virtue renders gentle, are well braced, firm, quick, and deep in feeling, touched by good and by evil, indulgent when they ought to be so, but without breaking the rules of duty. He who is naturally gentle, dares not reprove, lest he should become excited and lose his balance; he who is virtuously gentle, reproves energetically, but always with self-possession. One dissembles through timidity, the other speaks by the promptings of charity; one often runs the risk of failing in duty on this point; the other will always fulfil it faithfully without human respect; one spares others in order to spare himself: the other does so only for God's glory, and as the highest duty. But as to that gentleness which is merely politic, all real piety abhors the vice.

Cordiality is another produce of true religion. It was banished long ago from worldly intercourse, and its place was taken by politeness, which resembles it externally, dissembles its feelings, and affects those which it does not possess.

These demonstrations pass current; they are received and paid back in the same coin. But in reality no reliance is placed upon them, and they deceive no one who has the least experience. The first lesson taught by the world to its votaries is this: appear candid, but never be cordial. And the term itself is almost as little used in language as the thing signified, in society. Polite intercourse is reduced to vain and frequently derisive compliments; offers of service, the acceptance of which would be annoying; unmeaning promises, easily to be eluded at the time of fulfilment; assurances of good-will which always end in declarations of inability; and demonstrations of interest in others' concerns that are apparently vivid, but really cold, and often perfectly false.

How different is this external affectation from the cordiality of real Christians! Charity never fails in the requirements of true courtesy, but with them it combines frankness and candour; expresses only what it feels, and that, simply, unaffectedly, and persuasively. No evasion, no reticence, no affectation, all is thorough; love prompts speech, or discretion checks it. Sweet and safe and satisfying is intercourse with minds governed by charity. The multitude of the first Christians were "of one heart and of one soul," because they considered themselves members of one body, joined to one Head.

This unity is divine. Our LORD asked it from His Father in the night of His Passion: "That they all may be one; as Thou, Father art in Me, and I in Thee, that they also may be one in Us; that the world may believe that Thou hast sent Me." It is our LORD's will that the divine origin of His religion should be known by this sign. If unity reigned on earth, happiness would reign here likewise; and it was our LORD's mind that it should begin here and be perfected for ever in heaven. But where is it to be found now? In the hearts of a very small number of Christians, more rarely to be met with than is supposed. Generally the union of hearts is crossed by petty views of self-interest and self-seeking, which chill and hamper love, though they may not destroy its existence. Kindliness combined with cordiality, the disposition to take all in good part, which puts the best construction on everything, is not apt to take offence, not captious or suspicious—this state of feeling is not usual among persons professing devotion; they are often more inclined than others to judge severely, because they understand more, both about good and evil, and are endowed with more light to discern both in others.

Another fault common to such persons is that of esteeming themselves above others. Self-esteem and spiritual vanity are among the most dangerous snares which beset the entrance of the interior life. No sooner have you given yourself up to GOD, and fancied that you perceive a notable improvement in yourself, than you look at your neighbour, and measure yourself by him. You examine him from head to foot; you compare his conduct with your own; and what a wonderful difference you find! He has some fault from which, thank GOD, you are free; he does not practise some exercise which is habitual to you; he is not in the right way, where you fancy yourself to be walking almost alone; he runs into extremes, or is narrow-minded, or scrupulous. Your heart is fain to echo the words of the

Pharisee in the Gospel: "GOD, I thank Thee, that I am not as other men are."

These feelings are generally enhanced if any sensible sweetness has been felt at Communion; if emotion has wrung forth a few tears, then the soul fancies itself lifted altogether above this world, and gifted with eagles' wings for the loftiest of flights.

This is a subtle temptation, which it is difficult wholly to avoid, if GOD does not give a helping hand, by raising up some matter for humiliation, or by withdrawing His misused consolations. Spiritual pride is incomparably more to be feared than any other, because its objects are incomparably more excellent; therefore GOD visits those who yield to it with utter blindness, and its victims are exposed to certain ruin.

Those directors who have not the Spirit of GOD are thus apt to presume on their gifts, fancying themselves more enlightened than others: endued with a singular talent for the guidance of souls, which others understand nothing about. They are proud of the number and quality of their penitents; they use secret devices to increase their number. If they are not continually boasting of their own powers, that work is done for them by other lips. They express pity for those who apply to other priests, and imply that it is matter for regret that persons so well disposed should not have fallen into better hands. Therefore their first business, when a person submits to their direction, is to destroy the work that has been done by others, suggesting new methods, and insisting on the adoption of a different style. Directors of this kind have an intense spirit of domineering, and exercise despotic sway over souls. They do not bring them into subjection to grace, but to their own notions. They never tell them to hearken to the voice of GOD speaking in their own hearts; GOD is supposed to speak through their instrumentality alone, and any inward inspiration, not in accordance with their views, is to be treated as an illusion. I pray you, devout souls, to avoid these tyrants, and seek such persons as will watch the operations of grace in your soul, and conform their advice to it; their only method consisting in the lesson of attention and docility to the voice of the Good Shepherd.

The overlooking of our neighbours' faults is a fundamental rule of charity; severity with our own is the first principle of interior mortification. But many professed devotees assume the contrary as to both points. This always has been, and always will be, matter for regret.

How easy is that devotion which consists in blaming and critizing other people, sometimes with intolerable sharpness, sometimes with affectation of pity! Is that charity which can endure nothing, but ridicules all that we dislike, and is utterly intolerant with regard to manners, dispositions, and natural human imperfections? You need not flatter your neighbour on his unpleasant or reprehensible qualities; but you ought to bear with him, and not allow him to perceive that he is disagreeable to you.

With whom are you to live, if you will consort only with those that are faultless? By what rule of equity is it that you wish, not only that others should bear with you, but take pleasure in your company, and bend to your peculiarities, while you look upon your neighbour's as heavy burdens that you seek to shake off: complaining to one of the faults of another, and sparing nothing in any one? Do you think yourself faultless? If you feel that you need indulgence, be indulgent to others. Of all faults, intolerance to those of others is the most disagreeable.

"Bear ye one another's burdens, and so fulfil the law of CHRIST." This is a great art, most necessary in society, most conducive to the pleasantness of life.

S. John seems to reduce his whole system of morality to brotherly love and all-enduring charity. In extreme old age, when unable to preach at any length, he would cause himself to be carried into the congregation, and say only these words: "Little children, love one another." And when it was complained that he always repeated the same thing, he made answer: "It is the LORD'S commandment, and if this be fulfilled, it is sufficient." Now, of all the duties involved in this precept, the most essential is patient endurance, because its practice is continually needed, and the results are of the utmost consequence, whether it be fulfilled or neglected. Moreover, it is exceedingly difficult, because it demands continual care and unwearied efforts to subdue our own temper. Bearing all from others, and letting them have nothing to bear from us, is a mark of very great virtue.

But in order to reach this point, what a deadly war must be waged with our personal faults, and the self-love in which they are rooted! Say what we will, the true reason which makes us so fastidious with regard to our neighbour, is our own excessive self-love and self-esteem. The more we spare ourselves, the less we consider him. The blinder we are to our own imperfections, the more clear-sighted are we to those of others. The great and only means of becoming charitable, is the earnest practice of interior mortification, the application of knife and cautery to our own wounds, and the uprooting of the very feeblest fibre of unacknowledged self-complacency. As self-love dies, so will brotherly love be quickened.

But men will not receive this doctrine ; interior mortification is most distasteful to nature. The devout are ready to overload themselves with austerities, and pine for those they do not undertake ; they will fast immoderately, set about all practices of devotion, and spend many hours every day in prayer ; but few can make up their minds to repress ill-humour, stifle over-sensitiveness, check false suspicions, malicious curiosity, rash judgments, unjust prejudices : in fact, to make war against all bad habits ; and of those who do undertake this hard struggle, still fewer have the courage to carry it through to the end.

TWENTY-FIRST MAXIM.

Go straight on; never stop; never look back: grieve for sin, but never lose courage.

"*Forgetting those things which are behind, and reaching forth unto those things which are before, I press toward the mark for the prize of the high calling of God in Christ Jesus.*"

XXI.

OF PROGRESS.

ALL is not accomplished, when we have entered upon the ways of GOD; we must walk in them, and go ever onward; a refusal to advance is a consent to fall back, for it is impossible to stand still. GOD Himself sets us in the path of the inner life, regulates our speed, and causes some to advance more rapidly, and others more slowly. Our part is, in no wise to oppose His urging hand, or to retard our progress.

Now this progress is retarded, or wholly stopped in many ways, and by various causes which it is well to explain. It is retarded by cowardice, downheartedness, faithlessness, inconstancy, and many venial sins which show themselves in those who are not duly watchful.

Progress is altogether arrested by those who act like a traveller, who, instead of looking straight on, allows himself to be attracted by the objects that appear to right and left, and stands still to look at them. Observe, I do not mean that he leaves the road for the sake of such objects; that would be much worse, especially if, in order to enjoy them, he gave up the previous aim of his journey. Then we should not say that he stopped, but that he left his road altogether. I take it for granted that he remains in the right path, and that he intends to do so; but, fascinated by the beauty or novelty of the sights presented to his vision, he slackens his speed, or stops altogether in order to enjoy them at leisure; for while he gazes at them vaguely or slightly, without fixing his eyes or his mind upon them, the sight of them does not hinder his progress. This similitude is easy of application.

Those also stop who are perpetually looking to see where to set their foot; always trying to choose the best places, and going far round about to avoid awkward spots, instead of walking straight on, and running the risk of getting rather muddy. Nothing is more common than such precautions, hesitations, and deliberations in the path of the interior life. The pilgrim seeks certainty in order to avoid making any false step; wants to see where he is, fears over-fatigue, and is afraid of falling and getting a little soiled; he turns aside from difficult and slippery places, and from those that seem to threaten any danger. But grace says, Fear nothing, but go on; else the road will be lengthened, and perhaps the end will never be attained. Daintiness, cowardice, too great fear of the slightest falls, and of the least tarnishing of that purity of conscience which gratifies pride, cause disregard to the directions of grace, and prevent the soul from going on its road with full confidence in God, without inspecting it too narrowly, or taking such circuitous paths.

In a path so rough and uneven, with difficult passes scattered here and there, and precipices on both sides, why should we be so fearful of falls, and of the danger of soiling ourselves? when we ought to walk blindly under the safe conduct of faith, when such falls can only be slight and involuntary, and have only the effect of humbling us; and when GOD'S Hand is always ready to raise us again? Fear of death or of wounds never made a good soldier. We have a Physician Who can and will heal and quicken us. Why so greatly fear to expose ourselves by His orders, and under His mighty protection?

Again, the pilgrim stops, when, having accidentally fallen, instead of rising immediately, and setting forth with renewed energy, he lies stretched out on the ground, distressed, miserable, desponding by reason of his fall, and making no effort to rise; or again when, after having risen, he investigates the cause of his fall at great length and with inquisitive uneasiness, under the pretext of guarding against a similar accident on future occasions. This conduct implies great self-love, false discretion, and self-confidence.

He who walks on rapidly, or, still more, he who runs, is not so careful to see where he sets his foot; he climbs over all obstacles; he goes on deliberately, whether his path be impeded with ruts, or mire, or be overflowed with water; what matter to him that he is splashed, or muddy and wet, provided he makes progress? He is willing to expose himself to a few falls, in spite of which he leaves others far behind him. These accidents which he neither seeks nor fears, and are only caused by the impetuosity of his progress, never have any bad effect, but on the contrary, double his ardour; he rises quickly, and does not brood over his fall. GOD, towards Whom he is hastening, union with Whom he is eagerly seeking, is too merciful and too righteous to lay those faults to his account which are occasioned by the excessive confidence of entire surrender of self to Him, and of love for Him.

But all this is to be understood only of truly interior souls, of whom GOD has taken full and perfect possession, who are acted upon and urged by His Spirit; who abhor the least intentional fault, and the slightest resistance to grace, and who, moreover, have great courage, and are resolved on the most generous sacrifices. It would be wrong to apply this doctrine to ordinary souls, who, assisted by ordinary grace, advance by their own efforts in the path of virtue. These must always use prudent, though not anxious circumspection, they must keep an attentive watch over their steps, and be on their guard against all falls, and the more carefully, because their falls generally are wilful in a greater or less degree.

But, it will be said, how are we to make sure that we are advancing? You are to seek no such certainty; it is enough to know that you are not stopping, and this may be known by the witness of a quiet conscience, or by a peculiar peace, which in such a case is always present, even though unnoticed. In time of perplexity and darkness, this assurance is conveyed through the director, who answers to us for our own safety, soothes us, and bids us go on our way, leaning only upon faith and obedience.

I allow that faith is dark and obedience blind,

and that the assurance derived from them does not destroy the contrary impressions produced by imaginations and feeling. I grant that this assurance is neither bright nor absolute, nor does it bring with it a comforting conviction on which the soul may rest. But it is a kind of assurance which suits the trial; and while the trial lasts, no other must be expected, unless at few and momentary intervals.

What would be painful in this path if the soul were always certain that it was pleasing in GOD's sight? What sacrifice would there be? What proof would be given of trust and self-renunciation?

So then continual progress signifies that we go straight on, impelled by grace, and directed by obedience, knowing neither the road we tread nor the end to which it leads us; unconscious whether every action is pleasing to GOD, or will meet with reward. We must think of none of these things by our own free-will, and be simply absorbed by consideration of GOD's good pleasure and study of His will, which we may be sure of fulfilling if we do not fulfil our own.

But what is to be done, when instead of advancing we seem to be falling back? In this matter we must not defer to our own judgment, because there comes a time in the spiritual life at which the soul does not know its own state, and must not know it. This is the period in which we suppose ourselves yielding to temptation. We think ourselves cast off of GOD by reason of our sins, and imagine sin in every action. Are we therefore falling back? Far from it, we never were advancing more truly. Then we act with greater purity of intention; we intend self in nothing; we seek our own interests in no wise, either from creatures or from GOD. Then the most fatal blows are dealt to self-love, and it is reduced to the hardest straits; then we offer to GOD the sacrifice that glorifies Him most.

But we are not aware of our progress; every step seems to lead us toward the loss of all, and in a certain sense we verily lose ourselves; but we shall find ourselves again and for ever in GOD. This most blessed loss would never take place if we knew beforehand how it is to end. Therefore the experienced director of a soul in this state, is careful not to assure it of its safety with the desire of giving comfort. He emboldens it to self-sacrifice, but does not unveil the mystery of that sacrifice, nor the exceeding blessedness which will be its result. By doing so, he would hinder the work of GOD, and the perfection of the oblation.

This is the reason that, when this point is reached, GOD takes all means to prevent the thwarting of His work. Perhaps He removes the director, and sets in his place a person who understands nothing about the case; or, if He retains him, He closes his lips, and suffers him not to express what mistaken pity would have led him to declare; or, He allows him to be prejudiced, to turn against this soul and condemn it, and thus slay the victim with his own hands. These ineffable secrets of grace are known only by those who have experienced them, or are enlightened by GOD for the direction of others.

We will return to our maxim. It forbids us to look back. We look back when we regret what has been left for GOD'S sake, like the Israelites in the wilderness, who regretted the flesh-pots of Egypt, and loathed the manna which fell from heaven. In this sense our LORD declares: "No man having put his hand to the plough and looking back, is fit for the Kingdom of GOD." Even among men, regret for or resumption of a gift is looked on as contemptible, and only pardonable in a child who does not know what he is doing.

We look back when we retrace our steps in thought, and recal the past, in order curiously to scan the course of our religious life and the operations of the Spirit; which S. Paul condemns when, speaking of himself, he says: "This one thing I do; forgetting those things which are behind, and reaching forth unto those things which are before, I press toward the mark for the prize of the high calling of GOD in CHRIST JESUS."

We look back, when we are so attached to various means of perfection as to cling to them obstinately, or regret them inordinately, when it pleases GOD to deprive us of them; or when we cast longing eyes on a past state, preferring it to our present condition, in which nature has more to endure.

Again, we look back, when we are continually turning our head to see whether we are advancing, and have made much way. For as we do not see the goal before us, we can only judge of our progress by looking back to the point whence we started. Self-love inspires this curiosity, which does not obtain trustworthy information, and is followed by vain complacency, or else by despondency. The only effect of these considerations and retrospections, is the slackening or suspension of our progress, if indeed they do not cause us to turn back altogether.

Many souls are subject to this fault. Many

wish their director to tell them continually that they are going on well, and that he is pleased with their improvement. They say they do this in order to be strengthened and encouraged to greater efforts. Nonsense! Let them leave their director to tell them these things when he sees fit; for there are some times when he ought to keep up their courage. But generally they had better keep quiet, and believe that all is going on well, so long as they are not told the contrary.

Another fault, no less common and no less connected with self-love, is the being subject to uneasiness and distress at the slightest fault that escapes them, or the faintest proof of their own weakness. Those are masters of a great secret in the spiritual life, who know how to act aright with regard to the venial sins into which they fall, and how to turn them to account. We will consider this subject at some length.

I take for granted, in the first place, that a firm resolution has been made against the deliberate commission of any fault, however slight. A contrary mind seems incompatible with true devotion. By deliberate faults, I mean such as are committed habitually, consciously, without wish of correcting them, and without compunction, or without yielding to that contrition which grace excites in the soul. I am now speaking of none but venial sins, and want of responsiveness to grace. Now, the first thing that God puts into the heart of those whom He calls to the interior life, is a faithfulness which thoroughly follows out the inspirations of grace, and never intentionally acts contrary to the warning of conscience. And they very rarely commit such faults as these; if they did so they would soon fall from the state in which God has placed them.

Those faults, then, to which they are subject, are passing things, savouring of faint-heartedness, human respect, vanity, or curiosity; or else faults of quick temper, giddiness, inadvertence, indiscretion, peevishness, or impulse, which are rather imperfections of nature than decided faults.

The first counsel given on this subject by masters of the spiritual life is—never to be discouraged, whatever fault may have been committed, because self-inflicted discouragement arises only from self-love. We are startled at having fallen; we did not think ourselves capable of such a fault; as if a human being, who is nothing but corruption, weakness, and wickedness, ought to be surprised at his own lapses. Astonishment involves unacknowledged vexation, despondency, and a temptation to give everything up. Saints are humbled, but not discouraged, by their faults; they are not astonished at them; they would rather wonder that they commit no worse, knowing themselves to be what they are; and they constantly thank God that His goodness has so kept them aloof.

We partly cause this discouragement by allowing the imagination to brood over the fault committed; we magnify and exaggerate it, and make it into a monster, though it may be a mere trifle. Satan often interferes, too, in order to break down our courage, and induce us to miss our Communions, and cast us into perplexity.

To obviate these exertions of the imagination and their consequences, the second counsel is, to repent immediately on becoming aware of a fault, and then to dismiss it from the mind until the time for confession. Some persons think it right to be always thinking of their sins, carrying them about with them everywhere, keeping them constantly before their eyes. They are wrong. Such continual remembrance of their faults is only calculated to weaken and sadden them, and to hinder the proper discharge of their ordinary duties. They grow scrupulous, and are continually worrying their confessor.

The third counsel (and it is given by S. Francis de Sales) is to grieve for our faults with regard to God, Who is offended by them, and to rejoice over them on our own account, by reason of the humiliation they produce. By acting on this counsel, which pertains to great perfection, we should derive from our falls all the profit God intends when He permits them. According to the design of God, our daily offences are, so to speak, ingredients in the composition of our holiness. To the same end, when He wills, God makes use even of crimes and the greatest irregularities; as in the cases of David, Mary Magdalene, Mary Egyptiaca, and many other noble penitents. And why should not venial sins produce the same result, if we make use of them to acquire a knowledge of self, which is the most necessary of all knowledge, next to that of God?

Let us reserve the working out of this great truth for the next chapter.

TWENTY-SECOND MAXIM.

When we know our own helplessness, we learn to understand the value and efficacy of grace.

"*When I am weak, then am I strong.*"

XXII.

OF THE LIFE OF GRACE.

God's first aim in man's sanctification is His own glory. Although He commands us to do all that depends on us, He would have us acknowledge that we can do nothing of ourselves, that our attempts are vain, and our best resolutions fruitless, unless His grace prevent and follow all our good works; and that it is useless to try to build the temple of our holiness, except God begin and continue and finish the work, with our co-operation. Moreover (and this is S. Paul's express teaching) we are not able even to think a good thought; we have no idea of holiness, nor of what must be done to acquire it.

God is jealous of His glory, and He is minded that all true Christians shall learn these truths by their own experience. Thus they acquire humility, which is the mother of all other virtue, and without which virtue would but add to their condemnation, because tainted with pride. I say that these things are to be learned by experience; for what would it avail us to know that they are points of faith, if we had not an intimate sense of them which can be acquired by practice alone? And what would humility be, were it not rooted in a deep conviction of the soul arising from continual experience of its spiritual wretchedness?

God's dealings in this respect assume a more especially defined form with regard to those persons who lead an interior life. Of these He takes particular care, and is the more jealous concerning them, because they belong to Him by an unreserved donation and consecration. He leads them by the direct influence of His Spirit, He Himself assumes the task of their sanctification, He gives greater graces to them than to others; and therefore He would also have them learn more thoroughly that they are nothing, and can do nothing, that He provides for all things, works all good in them, and requires of them nothing but submission and obedience.

But how does He lead them to that sense of absolute and total powerlessness, and that perfect dependence on grace? First, He takes possession of their faculties, and does not allow the free use of them in spiritual matters. They feel as it were bound, and unable to exercise memory, understanding, or will, on any particular subject; He allows them no perception, no plan; if they conceive any design otherwise than by His inspiration, He disconcerts it. He takes from them every method and practice of their own choosing: He forbids every effort of their natural powers; He does not even permit them to endeavour, as others do, to acquire such or such a virtue, nor to use the ordinary means for that purpose. But He Himself assumes the task of governing and sanctifying them as He will, prescribing in due measure what they are to do or to avoid, infusing into their souls the habit of virtues, so that they cannot flatter themselves with the idea that they have in any degree attained them by their own exertions: they do not even know themselves to possess such virtues, and yet they act conformably to them in such circumstances and by such means as He pleases. This state is excessively annoying and humiliating to nature, very mortifying to self-love, and demanding, on the part of him who endures it, such fidelity as can only be maintained by great love and dauntless courage.

Secondly, He humbles them by the faults into which He suffers them to fall, particularly when He sees them relying on themselves, when they have made some good resolution on which they depend. These faults, indeed, are merely weakness; but it is just their own weakness of which He desires to make them conscious. Like a mother, who purposely leaves her child to himself, and lets him fall harmlessly, that he may understand his need of her, and learn to cling closely to her, because he cannot take a step alone without falling, nor rise alone after the fall.

These faults of pure frailty become more frequent, and apparently more considerable, in proportion to the progress made. Such or such a fault appeared to be cured, it now seems more dominant than ever; passions appeared to be overcome and brought under control, they are now violently rebellious. "The good that I would, I do not; but the evil which I would not, that I do. I delight in the law of GOD after the inward man; but I see another law in my members, warring against the law of my mind, and bringing me into captivity to the law of sin." After so many favours received from GOD, after so many protestations made to Him, this condition arouses deep shame in the soul which finds itself a prey to such misery, and it despairs of ever being able to conquer and correct itself.

In this sharp internal war between the old man and the new, in which the new man is apparently worsted, the soul is fain to cry: "O wretched man that I am! who shall deliver me from the body of this death?" By *this death* is understood this present life, which causes torture worse than death, and which is assumed to be a continual death to the life of grace. "All the violence I have used against myself, all my prayers, fastings, watchings, and austerities, have been of no avail against my enemy. Who then shall deliver me? It is out of my own power; I can add nothing to what I have done. The grace of JESUS CHRIST my LORD will set me free." Nothing else has the power to work so great a marvel.

To this confession of the power of grace and the powerlessness of the human will, it is GOD'S intention to reduce the soul. It is His will that His deliverance should be acknowledged as a free gift, with which it has had nothing to do except to wait for it trustfully. Thus GOD glorifies Himself in such a soul, leaving it no support in its own strength, and, by the sense of its sufferings, and its vain efforts to rid itself of them, obliging it to acknowledge that the cure is due to the heavenly Physician alone.

Therefore let us accept GOD'S will concerning us; and let us cause our faults, and temptations, and the sense of our own wretchedness to redound to His glory, by the humiliation they bring upon us, by the acknowledgment of our powerlessness, and by perfect confidence in His loving-kindness. We will grieve, but not despond. Sorrow comes from GOD: despondency arises from self-love. We will humble ourselves, patiently, quietly, placidly. We will despair of ourselves; but we will expect everything from GOD. He will come and help us; but not till, weary, exhausted, and convinced of the futility of all else, we turn to Him alone.

Ordinary Christians do feel the value of grace; but as they superadd their own ingenuity, and GOD blesses their labour, they do not feel its full value. In like manner, when they commit any fault, they are humbled; but at the same time they are aware that it was in their power to resist; they bear witness to themselves that they fought first, and yielded afterwards. Therefore their falls are quite voluntary; and they see that it depends on themselves to rise, that grace presses them to do so, and that they do not heed, because they will not heed; and so they have not a perfect knowledge of their own weakness. How should they, when they are always conscious of their active strength, even in their very falls? These are men who have the free use of their faculties.

It is not so with interior souls, when they have entered the passive way; these are absolutely children, to whom GOD allows no feeling but that of their own weakness, and who are strong only in His strength. But it must be remembered that this point is only reached after their active strength has been exhausted in all manner of practices, internal and external. For it would be a great illusion to imagine that GOD shows the slightest favour to laziness, indolence, and inaction.

In this state of infancy, if they act aright, grace so acts with them, that there is no sensible labour on their part, because they are deprived of all natural activity. Yet they do co-operate, but with a co-operation, as it were, imperceptible to themselves, the principle of which lies in their having yielded up their free will to GOD, to be disposed of according to His will. They are borne onwards in the path of perfection, as a child is carried in its mother's arms, but not till after they have voluntarily cast themselves into the arms of GOD, from Whom they would not part for worlds. They do not use both sails and oars, as others do; the wind alone fills their sails and drives them on: this comparison is S. Theresa's. Now, he who rows, contributes to his progress by his own labour, and has a right to attribute it, in some part, to himself. But he who is carried on by the wind alone, cannot doubt that he is wholly indebted to it; all he has to do is to unfurl the sail, to catch the wind, and allow himself to be driven unresistingly. Thus, in the passive state, the full value and efficacy of grace are more truly appreciated.

Souls in this state have likewise a keener and deeper feeling of their weakness in the faults to which they give way, because they do give way through weakness only. They do not choose to commit such faults; they make the most earnest resolutions against them; they multiply prayers and austerities; and yet they fall; and GOD only suffers it in order to humble and annihilate them in their own eyes. Let me repeat that I do not speak of great faults: a soul that falls into such sins, must previously have withdrawn itself from GOD. But as long as they faithfully continue yielded up to Him, as long as they do not intentionally allow themselves in the slightest imperfection, and relax no exercise of piety, their falls are inconsiderable in themselves; they are exterior and apparent only; for the will has no share in them. They may say, like S. Paul: "It is no more I that do it, but sin that dwelleth in me." And that root of sin, which they unsuccessfully endeavour to destroy, fills them with shame, and with a holy horror of self, especially as they suppose themselves to consent to what passes within them, though they are very far from doing so. And GOD does not place them in a state so humiliating and crucifying to nature, until they are far advanced, and their will is, so to speak, confirmed in well-doing by long practice.

Among interior persons, nothing is more real, nor more common than this state, though it be inexplicable; and if directors do not understand it, they are liable to make great mistakes, which may cast such souls into a state of despair. They certainly do not wish to sin, and they do all that in them lies to avoid sinning; and yet things escape them which are apparently sinful; they reproach and accuse themselves of these things, as of so many sins. If the confessor, then, imprudently agreed with them, and declared that they had sinned, he would distress them, drag them down to despair, and cause them to run the risk of losing their senses, or of destroying themselves. Sad examples of this kind have been known.

What then must he do? He must enter into the intention of GOD, Whose will it is to slay self-love in these souls, and to let them find no help in themselves, either for doing good, or avoiding evil. They may declare that their consent was given to sin: but the confessor must beware of giving credit to their asseverations; for some time he should tell them boldly that they did not consent: he should then reduce them to simply saying what they have felt, without allowing them to call it sin; and oblige them to submit their judgment to his, and to draw near the holy Altar, in spite of repugnance and terror. Never were such souls more pure, than when they thus think themselves covered with sins: never were they more humble, obedient, dead to self-will, diffident concerning themselves. There are so many certain marks upon them of GOD's guidance, that a man must be very enlightened if he does not acknowledge them, or very timid and irresolute, if he does not yield to them. In such a case, it would be his plain duty to give up the task of directing such persons, and to advise their applying to some other priest.

TWENTY-THIRD MAXIM.

Love is our law; God is our portion: here by faith; there by sight.

"*Now abideth faith, hope, charity, these three; but the greatest of these is charity. Charity never faileth.*

XXIII.

OF LOVE.

THE Christian law is a law of love: it is all comprised in the love of GOD. We are bound to love Him for Himself, and to love ourselves in Him, and our neighbour for Him. GOD is the one principle, and aim, and end of all; and love, says S. Augustine, is the only worship He exacts and accepts. Faith, alone, does not honour Him: the devils believe and tremble. Hope without love is insufficient, because it pauses at GOD's promises without advancing to Himself. Charity, only, reaches Him, is united to Him, and rests in Him as in supreme Good. What avails the practice of exterior works, if not animated and quickened by the heart? Men pay attention to demonstrations, and judge of the heart by them, because they cannot look deeper. But GOD looks upon the heart: and according to the state of the heart He values all things else.

Love is the only feeling which makes our LORD's yoke easy to us, and His burden light.

Fear causes us to feel the whole weight of the law: hope lightens it but in part: love alone bids it disappear. "Who loves, labours not," says S. Augustine. Love always fears not doing enough, counts what it does as nothing, and aspires to do more. Love knows no bounds: it is always susceptible of increase, especially if its object is infinitely lovely. Love of such an object is at once a motive and a means for loving it more. The more it is beloved, the better it is known: and the better it is known, the more one would fain love it: so that knowledge and love increase each other to infinity.

The soul enjoys the true liberty of the sons of God, only in so far as it loves. "Love," says S Augustine again, "and do what you will." You will never will anything contrary to love, nor, therefore, contrary to a law wholly based on love. S. Paul speaks in this sense when he says that the law is not made for a righteous man. Wherein does he need an external law? Its precepts are all written on his heart. There he finds not only the law, but the perfection of the law. For love suffers him not to stop short at the things God commands: it urges him on to those which please Him, and which He counsels, without expressly commanding. Love is his rule, his bias and his measure; and in obeying it he does simply what it would grieve him not to do. Therefore, he is thoroughly free: for liberty consists in doing what we will, and in willing what we do.

This love is purer, in proportion as the heart becomes more detached from its own interests, and tends towards the object it loves, without looking back on itself. This purity of love is the point to which God continually strives to raise the soul that has given itself to Him: favours, and trials, and sacrifices, all combine to purify its love, and cleanse it from all alloy: so that the interior way may be defined as a state, not of pure love, but of continual tendency towards pure love.

It may be said that the tending towards pure love is also the aim of the ordinary way; and I am willing to allow it. But pray observe the difference. In the ordinary way, man retains the command of his liberty, and mingles his own action with the operation of GOD; which hinders that operation from producing its full effect; but in the passive or interior way, man having yielded to GOD all right over his own free will, GOD acts upon him more powerfully; nothing clogs or restrains His operation, and therefore it unfolds its full efficacy. It is difficult, not to say impossible, for this difference to be understood by those who are not in the passive way, however perfect they may be in other respects. But it is none the less real; and it would be presumptuous to doubt the word of Saints who have spoken on this matter from their own experience.

Moreover, we are not to take fright at the mention of pure love, as though it were contrary to Christian hope. Those who have so written as to give rise to this idea have expressed themselves incorrectly or been misunderstood. In this life charity does not, and never can, exclude hope. As long as we do not possess the thing we love, we desire to do so; and not only desire it, but hope for it, in virtue of GOD's promises; and we count it a duty to hope for it, by reason of the express command He lays on all His children.

Charity, on earth, always implies the two other theological virtues; and, far from destroying them, perfects them while it perfects itself. Anything, destructive of faith or hope, would be still more destructive of charity. So that it is absurd to suppose that trials whose object is to purify love, can in the least degree weaken hope. Faith, hope, and charity abide in the greatest Saints till the end of their pilgrimage. Then faith ceases, because they no longer believe, but see; hope fades out, because they possess, or are certain of possessing; charity reigns alone, because in heaven there is scope for charity only. This is S. Paul's teaching, and it is grounded on the very essence and definition of the three virtues.

Nothing contrary to this is proved by the sacrifices to which God moves the soul in a state of extreme trial. By such trial, God does not intend to purify love to the detriment of hope; in so doing, He would be acting contrary to Himself; but, while purifying love, He intends at the same time to purify hope, and to lead the soul to set His will and His glory above all selfish interest; and this does not require the soul to renounce happiness, but to make it duly subordinate to the good pleasure of God.

Perhaps it would have been better if no one had treated of these matters. They are extremely delicate, and it is very difficult to set them forth, or even to understand them, with perfect precision. It is not necessary to be acquainted with them beforehand, because God calls very few to such great sacrifice; and those whom He does call, are then in such a state of perplexity and darkness that they can make no use of previous knowledge. As to the directors of such souls, God never fails to teach them the right method of guidance, provided they consult Him in prayer;

and the best books would be useless to them, if they did not learn to understand them by their own union with GOD. But, as this subject, which is the highest of all relating to the interior life, was much brought into notice about the beginning of the last century, and, in consequence of a very just condemnation, many persons became prejudiced against things understood by few, I have thought fit to explain the matter briefly, in order to correct false impressions, and to dispel prejudice.

The great and priceless advantage of love is, that it leads us to the eternal possession of GOD; and this is the privilege of love alone. Faith and hope cannot open the gate of heaven, if charity be not joined with them. Even during this life, love enables us to possess GOD, in a certain sense; for loving Him is the beginning of possessing Him. We may love any other object without possessing it, or possess it without loving it. But GOD, the Supreme Good, has this especial attribute: that His love cannot be separated from His fruition, nor His fruition from His love.

Of course such fruition is imperfect on earth, because it takes place beneath the veil of faith. But the heart delights in GOD, and is filled with Him, and contemns everything else; and if it have yet any desire left, it can only be that of a fuller and surer enjoyment. Yes: when the love of GOD reaches a certain point, it stills all the agitations of the human heart, even in this life; it brings peace, which cannot be broken, so long as that love subsists which gave it birth.

But who are those in whom love rises to such a degree as to give them in their exile a foretaste of the happiness of Home? Chiefly interior souls;

those who are especially sons of GOD, because led by His Spirit, and who, as sons, already have some share in their Father's inheritance. Others share His gifts and graces; these enter on an anticipative fruition of the Divine Essence. Having given themselves wholly to GOD, GOD gives Himself likewise to them; He binds them to Himself; He communicates to them the changelessness of peace and rest which He hath in Himself.

And the proof of this is, that no earthly events, whatever, cause them joy or sorrow; they accept all things with an even mind, and though some slight agitation may take place on the surface, the depth of the soul is always imperturbable. I appeal to the experience of the Saints. Were souls ever seen more calm and well balanced? Look at their serenity in the midst of torture. Is it the effect of their reflections, and of efforts for self-control made at such moments? No: they owe it to the possession of GOD, Who so fills their hearts, that He leaves no access for alien feeling, or for any thought of self.

TWENTY-FOURTH MAXIM.

Let us pray that these lessons may redound to the greater glory of God, and the greater blessedness of our own souls.

"*Thus have I looked for Thee in holiness, that I might behold Thy power and glory; for Thy loving-kindness is better than the life itself.*"

XXIV.

THE CONCLUSION OF THE WHOLE MATTER.

THE words which form the heading of this chapter are not shaped as a maxim; but yet they contain three great truths, by the explanation of which I intend to close this volume.

The first is, that by prayer we may attain to be numbered amongst interior souls: the second, that such souls glorify GOD more than others: the third, that they are by far the most happy.

I suppose myself addressing one, who, having read or heard somewhat concerning the interior life, feels a keen longing to live that divine life. The longing manifestly comes from GOD, and is itself the beginning of that which it seeks. Keep the spark a-light by fervent assiduous prayer; offer yourself heartily to GOD, not once in a way, but every day, and many times a day; pray Him to open the way to that promised land; with the end of obtaining this grace, communicate, do good works, fulfil the duties of your station, suffer its troubles; and you surely will obtain your request. For God does not plant such a desire in a Christian heart, to leave it unfruitful; if you are eager in the pursuit of this blessing, God is the inspirer of your eagerness; if you do all in your power to obtain it, God is stirring you up, and giving you courage and perseverance. Therefore you will obtain what you ask, provided you go on asking, and faint not. Could God reject a soul that desires to be all His own, and that only desires this so far as He gives it the good will?

But yet be careful not to heat your imagination, and not to be impatient and excited in your pursuit; pray peacefully, and peacefully await the effect of your prayer. God has fixed His time for answering it; seek not to hurry His work.

On the other hand, coldness, and negligence, and indifference in prayer, would prove that you neither knew nor desired the blessing you asked.

But if you pray aright, God will take possession of your soul at last, either suddenly, or gradually. If suddenly, you will feel at that moment a perfect assurance of it, by reason of the immediate change which will take place in you. If gradually, then follow the workings of grace step by step, and be extremely faithful; for all depends on that. Once in the way, you have but to walk in it, directed within by the Spirit of God, and without by your spiritual guide.

Most Christians receive some touch of the interior life; when, for instance, they return to God, after going astray, it may be, for a long time; grace always tends to that aim. If they could or would nourish that spark: if directors, themselves interior, would take the pains needful for its development, the effect of such efforts would soon be seen; and there would so be very little difficulty about the matter, in its first beginnings. Most obstacles arise from false or imperfect ideas of a devout life, which is supposed to involve many practices, and methods, and much activity, and a great deal of self and self-will. They arise, too, from habits of serving GOD according to a fixed plan, which restrains the operations of grace; (and it is scarcely possible for persons of mature age to overcome such habits:) from prejudices against the interior life, which is held to be an extraordinary and dangerous way, liable to many illusions. And lastly, from directors themselves, who, for these reasons, or to save themselves trouble, or for fear of losing reputation, bar the entrance of the interior life from those who are under their guidance.

If all these persons were actuated by zeal for GOD's interest, they would think very differently; for it is certain that we cannot glorify Him more, than by dedicating ourselves completely to Him, that He may lead us as He will. Indeed, GOD then glorifies Himself, in the soul wherein He finds no resistance. And shall we doubt that He glorifies Himself in the most excellent manner, and according to the whole scope of His designs, so soon as the creature offers no opposition? Will and power are both His own: nothing but human liberty can impede the working of His power; and that impediment ceases to exist, when liberty is freely yielded up into GOD's hands.

Moreover, the glory of GOD lies in the free subjection of our will to His. Therefore, if that subjection is absolute, extending to all points, continuous and never broken, the glory GOD derives from it is as great as is possible for it to be; for His creature can offer Him nothing beyond it.

God is glorified by our sanctification. The more He acts in a soul by grace, the more that soul is sanctified. But, in what soul does God act more freely, more efficaciously, and more independently, than in that which has constituted Him ruler of its faculties, keeping them continually submissive to His will, and only reserving for itself a constant attention to His guidance, and an exact fidelity in following it? If it persevere to the end in this disposition, is it not clear that God will raise it to that degree of holiness which He intends for it, and that He will derive all the glory He requires from it?

Moreover, they glorify God, who see Him alone in everything; who refer all to Him; look to His interests only; consider their own as subordinate; receive good and evil at His hands with an even mind, and bless His Name for all things. But this is done by a soul which leads the interior life. Its eye, that is, its intention, is single, pure, ever turned towards God; no lower view or interest defiles it. Such a soul is in a state of holy indifference respecting what befals it; all that it receives from God is welcome, because sent by God: it is as well contented to bear all manner of crosses and trials, as to be loaded with good things; because the only thing it holds to be good, is the will of God.

Last of all, the glory God derives from these souls in heaven, is proportionate to that which they have rendered Him on earth. Then, perfected in love, rapt in the vision of Him to Whom they gave themselves, when as yet they knew Him but by faith, they will for ever offer Him an unimaginable tribute of adoration, thanksgiving, praise, and love. As their sacrifice of themselves was peculiarly conformed to the sacrifice of CHRIST, so GOD will thence receive an especial glory, of the same kind as that which He receives from the sacred Humanity of His Only Begotten SON. We may be sure of this, that there will be no comparison between this glory and that which He will receive from the rest of the elect.

But the glory rendered by the creature to its Creator, is the rule and measure of its own felicity. Judge then, if it be possible, what beatitude will be the portion of these souls in heaven. All I can say is, that GOD will give Himself to them as they gave themselves to Him. But they gave themselves to Him without any reserve, with the whole of their heart. Therefore GOD will spare nothing in rewarding them. They gave themselves to Him, weak, poor, imperfect creatures: He will give Himself to them, Almighty GOD, infinitely great, and generous, and glorious. They loved Him but as creatures, and according to the narrow capacity of their hearts; He will love them as GOD, with a love as far beyond their own, as the Uncreated Essence is beyond the being formed from nothing. If I dare say so, He will be devoted and dedicated to them, as they were to Him. He will render them all for all: an unbounded, infinite All, for an all limited and finite. Others among the blessed ones gave with measure, and will receive with measure. These gave without measure, and will receive without measure. Merciful justice will regulate the reward of the former: pure, generous, lavish love will rule the reward of the latter. Its profusion would exhaust the riches of GOD, were they not inexhaustible. Such happiness awaits them in heaven.

Who shall doubt that these souls, while yet on earth, are happy, so far as the conditions of this life allow? What is happiness, but the love and possession of sovereign good? But they do love sovereign good: even in this life they possess it according to the full capacity of their heart: GOD fills it, and leaves no room for any other desire. They are neither attracted nor flattered by earthly honours or gratifications; they enjoy a blessing which leads them to despise all things else. Does this blessing consist in the gifts and favours of GOD? By no means. They receive them gratefully, when it pleases Him to bestow them; but they do not long for them, nor cling to them, nor do they fret at being deprived of them. The blessing they possess is GOD Himself, and He is infinitely beyond all His gifts.

Again; what is happiness? Peace of heart. But such peace is always theirs. Intense, changeless, untouched by feelings, independent of vicissitudes both of the natural and spiritual life; abiding in the depth of the heart, despite all trial and temptation; bound up with the very crosses which they bear, and without which they would not wish to live. This is past all understanding, but it is true.

Would you know whether these souls are happy? Ask them if anything in the world would induce them to wish themselves otherwise situated, to desire alleviation of their sufferings, to move from under the rule of the Divine will: if they even wish GOD to relieve them and end their pain. They will answer, No; they are satisfied, and their desires are fulfilled, provided GOD glorifies Himself in them as He will. Show me any other happiness on earth to be compared with this. There is none. That of innocence is great; that of true, loving penitence is great likewise; that of ordinary Christian holiness is still greater. But that of souls sanctified by GOD Himself in the interior way of bare faith and self-abnegation is above all. We must needs be in that way, in order to believe this; but when we have advanced some distance in it, we doubt no longer.

LONDON:
SWIFT AND CO., REGENT PRESS, KING STREET,
REGENT STREET, W.

Printed in the USA
CPSIA information can be obtained
at www.ICGtesting.com
LVHW022049020124
767839LV00012B/663